Grade 7

Addison-Wesley Mathematics

Practice Workbook

▲▲ Addison-Wesley Publishing Company

Menlo Park, California ■ Reading, Massachusetts ■ New York
Don Mills, Ontario ■ Wokingham, England ■ Amsterdam ■ Bonn
Sydney ■ Singapore ■ Tokyo ■ Madrid ■ San Juan

ISBN 0-201-27703-4

ABCDEFGHIJKL-HC-96543210

Table of Contents

Name _____

Number and Place Value

Write the numeral.

1. five hundred seventy-six _____

2. nine thousand, six hundred fifty-nine _____

3. twenty-three thousand, two hundred twelve _____

4. six hundred fifty-five thousand, nine hundred nine _____

5. eight million, two hundred thousand, six hundred six _____

6. fourteen billion, nineteen thousand, fifteen _____

Write each standard numeral in words.

7. 2,341 _____

8. 19,862 _____

9. 205,205 _____

10. 8,400,021 _____

11. 7,000,006,002 _____

Write each number using expanded notation.

12. 4,321 _____

13. 456,007 _____

14. 73,200,105 _____

15. 6,050,203,098

Relating the Operations

Create an addition problem for each subtraction problem.

Example: $24 - 8 = 16 \rightarrow 16 + 8 = 24$ or $8 + 16 = 24$

1. $17 - 9 = 8$

_____

2. $27 - 12 = 15$

_____

3. $35 - 11 = 24$

_____

4. $43 - 29 = 14$

_____

Create an addition problem for each multiplicaton problem.

Example: $6 \times 9 = 54 \rightarrow 9 + 9 + 9 + 9 + 9 + 9 = 54$

5. $4 \times 12 = 48$

_____

6. $5 \times 23 = 115$

_____

7. $7 \times 5 = 35$

_____

8. $3 \times 14 = 42$

_____

Create a subtraction problem for each division problem.

Example: $42 \div 21 = 2 \rightarrow 42 - 21 - 21 = 0$

9. $69 \div 23 = 3$

_____

10. $24 \div 6 = 4$

_____

11. $35 \div 7 = 5$

_____

12. $114 \div 57 = 2$

_____

Create a multiplication problem for each division problem.

Example: $75 \div 3 = 25 \rightarrow 3 \times 25 = 75$ or $25 \times 3 = 75$

13. $64 \div 16 = 4$

_____

14. $72 \div 8 = 9$

_____

15. $81 \div 9 = 9$

_____

16. $108 \div 27 = 4$

_____

Name _____

Order of Operations

Follow the order of operations to evaluate each expression.

1. $7 - 3 + 6$ _____

2. $16 + 29 - 8$ _____

3. $38 - 12 - 17$ _____

4. $22 + 18 + 71$ _____

5. $(20 \div 10) + 3$ _____

6. $14 + (7 \times 6)$ _____

7. $(56 \div 28) \times 5 + 17$ _____

8. $(16 \times 4) - (4 \times 15)$ _____

9. $18 - (12 \div 3) + 6$ _____

10. $(96 \div 16) \times 3$ _____

11. $27 - (16 \div 8) \times 13$ _____

12. $22 + (3 \times 3 - 6)$ _____

13. $49 \div (56 \div 8) - 4$ _____

14. $18 \times (13 - 11) \div 6$ _____

15. $35 \div 5 + (18 - 14)$ _____

16. $21 \div (15 - 12) \times 5$ _____

17. $28 - 6 \times (8 - 7)$ _____

18. $(30 \div 15) + (4 \times 7)$ _____

19. $(17 - 9) \div 2 - 3$ _____

20. $18 - (6 \div 3 \times 4)$ _____

21. $33 - (16 \times 2) + 7$ _____

22. $14 \div (36 - 29) + 11$ _____

23. $56 \div 2 \div (2 \times 7)$ _____

24. $29 - (18 \div 3 \times 4)$ _____

25. $5 + (9 \times 4) - 12$ _____

26. $(9 - 3) \times 5 - 17$ _____

27. $15 \div (8 \div 2 + 1)$ _____

28. $90 - (15 \times 4) - 8$ _____

29. $(19 - 14 \div 2) \div 4$ _____

30. $(4 + 5) \times 5 - 6$ _____

31. $10 - (16 - 4 \times 3)$ _____

32. $32 - (15 + 6)$ _____

33. $22 - (13 - 7) \div 2$ _____

34. $28 - (3 + 6) \times 3$ _____

Write each operation sign ($+$, $-$, $\times$, $\div$) one time to
get the indicated value. Use parentheses when needed.

35. 6 ___ 5 ___ 12 ___ 6 ___ $2 = 5$

36. 4 ___ 2 ___ 8 ___ 1 ___ $5 = 43$

Problem Solving: Introduction

Circle the statement or statements that indicate how to
solve each problem.

1. Note cards are on sale, 2 boxes for
$3.88. How much would 5 boxes cost?

  A Multiply 3.88 by 2; then divide the
     product by 5.

  B Divide 3.88 by 2; then multiply the
     quotient by 5.

  C Multply 3.88 by 5; then add 2.

2. A punch recipe makes 48 servings.
How many people were served if each
person drank 2 servings and there were
6 servings left over?

  A Divide 48 by 2; then subtract 6 from
     the quotient.

  B Multiply 6 by 2; then subtract the
     product from 48.

  C Subtract 6 from 48; then divide the
     difference by 2.

3. Eggs cost $1.18 a dozen. How much
would 36 eggs cost?

  A Divide 1.18 by 36.

  B Divide 36 by 12; then multiply the
     quotient by 1.18.

  C Divide 1.18 by 12; then multiply the
     quotient by 3.

4. One door prize was awarded for every
18 people attending the meeting. How
many prizes were awarded if 90 people
attended the meeting?

  A Divide 90 by 18.

  B Subtract 18 from 90.

  C Divide 90 by 18; then multiply by 5.

5. In a survey, 1,530 people liked science
fiction movies. Twice as many people
did not like them. How many people
were surveyed?

  A Multiply 1,530 by 2.

  B Multiply 1,530 by 2; then add the
     product to 1,530.

  C Multiply 1,530 by 3.

6. There are 600 students at Dayton
School. Out of every 100 students, 75
are planning to attend the pep rally.
How many students are planning to
attend the pep rally?

  A Divide 600 by 75; then multiply the
     quotient by 100.

  B Divide 600 by 100; then divide the
     quotient by 75.

  C Divide 600 by 100; then multiply
     the quotient by 75.

Using Critical Thinking

Complete the flowcharts below.

1.

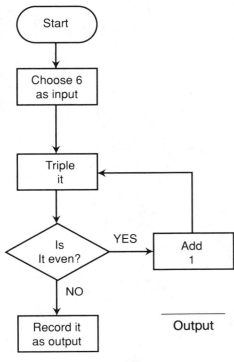

2.

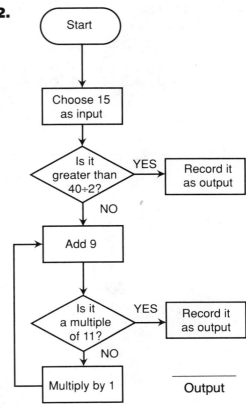

3.

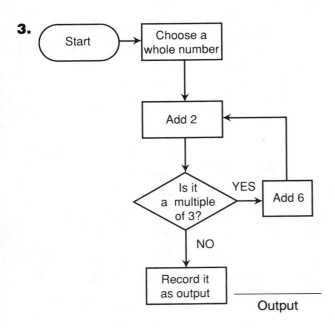

4.

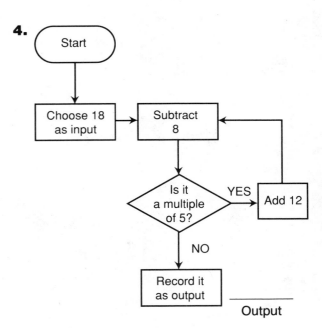

Basic Properties

Name the property used.

1. $46 \times 62 = 62 \times 46$

_____

2. $271 \times 1 = 271$

_____

3. $(3 \times 7) + (3 \times 2) = 3 \times (7 + 2)$

_____

4. $(8 \times 5) \times 4 = 8 \times (5 \times 4)$

_____

5. $1 \times 4{,}563 = 4{,}563$

_____

6. $(4 \times 51) + 4(6) = 4 \times (51 + 6)$

_____

7. $73 + 12 = 12 + 73$

_____

8. $2{,}727 + 0 = 2{,}727$

_____

9. $7 \times (50 + 3) = (7 \times 50) + (7 \times 3)$

_____

10. $9 + (7 + 2) = (9 + 7) + 2$

_____

Use the basic properties to find the value of n.

11. $44 \times 28 = n \times 44$

$n = \underline{\hspace{1cm}}$

12. $9(4 + 3) = (9 \times n) + (9 \times 3)$

$n = \underline{\hspace{1cm}}$

13. $5 \times (7 \times 6) = (5 \times 7) \times n$

$n = \underline{\hspace{1cm}}$

14. $652 + n = 652$

$n = \underline{\hspace{1cm}}$

15. $n \times (8 + 9) = (5 \times 8) + (5 \times 9)$

$n = \underline{\hspace{1cm}}$

16. $3 \times (n \times 8) = (3 \times 9) \times 8$

$n = \underline{\hspace{1cm}}$

17. $n \times 1 = 93$

$n = \underline{\hspace{1cm}}$

18. $n + 72 = 72 + 60$

$n = \underline{\hspace{1cm}}$

19. $(n \times 4) \times 2 = 6 \times (4 \times 2)$

$n = \underline{\hspace{1cm}}$

20. $(6 \times 3) + (6 \times 4) = n \times (3 + 4)$

$n = \underline{\hspace{1cm}}$

Name _____

Mental Math Techniques

Evaluate using mental math. Count on or back.

1. $3 + 128 =$ _____

2. $79 + 20 =$ _____

3. $301 - 30 =$ _____

4. $596 + 30 =$ _____

5. $121 - 3 =$ _____

6. $214 + 20 =$ _____

7. $849 + 2 =$ _____

8. $208 + 3 =$ _____

Evaluate using mental math. Use compatible numbers.

9. $8 + 53 + 2 =$ _____

10. $\$1.50 + \$0.79 + \$0.50 =$ _____

11. $8 \times 50 \times 100 =$ _____

12. $4 \times 88 \times 25 =$ _____

13. $15 + 75 + 10 =$ _____

14. $98 + 567 + 2 =$ _____

15. $80 + 345 + 20 =$ _____

16. $130 - 6 - 8 - 4 =$ _____

17. $256 - 11 - 6 - 9 =$ _____

18. $2 \times 33 \times 5 =$ _____

19. $6 \times 20 \times 10 =$ _____

20. $8 + 25 + 2 =$ _____

21. $\$2.92 + \$5.00 + \$0.08 =$ _____

22. $125 + 45 + 5 =$ _____

23. $90 + 335 + 10 =$ _____

Name _____

Choosing Estimation Techniques

Estimate. Use compatible numbers.

1. $36 + 33 =$ _____

2. $53 - 14 =$ _____

3. $59 + 14 =$ _____

4. $381 - 78 =$ _____

5. $5,999 \times 9 =$ _____

6. $525 - 124 =$ _____

7. $39.99 + 14.99 =$ _____

8. $980 - 221 =$ _____

9. $28 + 11 =$ _____

10. $82 \times 19 =$ _____

11. $3,501 + 298 =$ _____

12. $491 - 92 =$ _____

13. $646 + 18 =$ _____

14. $21 + 780 =$ _____

15. $23 + 76 =$ _____

16. $2,800 \div 15 =$ _____

Estimate. Use rounding.

17. $596 - 501 =$ _____

18. $295 \times 12 =$ _____

19. $796 \times 105 =$ _____

20. $52 \times 17 =$ _____

21. $32 \times 56 =$ _____

22. $18 \times 19 =$ _____

23. $48 \times 61 =$ _____

24. $88 \times 23 =$ _____

25. $81 \times 14 =$ _____

26. $305 \times 802 =$ _____

27. $490 + 111 =$ _____

28. $1,712 \times 9 =$ _____

Name _____

Problem Solving: Developing a Plan

Decide if you need an exact answer or an estimate.
Explain.

1. You are going shopping for a new pair of running
shoes. You ask a friend how much her shoes cost.

_____

_____

2. You bought a record and paid with a $10 bill.
How much change should you receive?

_____

_____

3. You are listening to the record, but you promised
your sister you would play tennis with her. She
wants to know how long the record is.

_____

_____

4. Your family is filling out income tax forms and
wants to know how much they owe the
government.

_____

_____

Solve. Tell whether you chose mental math, paper
and pencil, or calculator.

5. $568 - 234 =$ _____   **6.** $150 + 68 + 150 =$ _____

_____   _____

7. $200 \div 8 =$ _____   **8.** $2.753 + 24.56 =$ _____

_____   _____

Variables and Algebraic Expressions

Complete each table by evaluating the expressions.

1.

m	$m + 8$
6	
9	
12	
22	
64	

2.

y	$y - 6$
9	
15	
24	
32	
47	

3.

b	$3 \times b$
5	
10	
13	
21	
35	

4.

s	$\dfrac{s}{2}$
6	
18	
24	
34	
48	

5.

n	$n + 12$
4	
10	
12	
31	
57	

6.

c	$10 \times c$
8	
15	
27	
59	
82	

Evaluate each expression for $c = 5$, $d = 2$, $e = 7$.

7. $9 \times d$ _____

8. $7 + (2 \times e)$ _____

9. $(2 \times d) + e$ _____

10. $75 \times d$ _____

11. $(12 \times e) \div 6$ _____

12. $8 \times c$ _____

13. $(e - c) + 9$ _____

14. $12 - (c + e)$ _____

15. $30 \div c$ _____

16. $18 \times c$ _____

17. $(39 + c) - e$ _____

18. $(3 \times c) - 15$ _____

Name _____

Understanding Decimals

Write each number in standard form.

1. forty-five and two hundred thirty-five thousandths _____

2. seventeen and one thousand three hundred five ten-thousandths _____

3. four and three thousandths _____

4. sixty-three hundredths _____

5. one thousand and one thousandth _____

6. one hundred forty and seventeen ten-thousandths _____

7. ten and seven hundred seventy-seven ten-thousandths _____

8. eighteen and four hundredths _____

9. four hundred forty-four and four hundred forty-four thousandths _____

10. sixty-two and five thousand three hundred fifty-nine ten-thousandths _____

11. thirty-nine ten-thousandths _____

Compare the decimals by writing >, <, or = for each ◯.

12. 0.6 ◯ 0.7

13. 0.89 ◯ 0.83

14. 9.32 ◯ 9.35

15. 6.29 ◯ 6.32

16. 12.3334 ◯ 12.3342

17. 6.3 ◯ 6.30

18. 0.33 ◯ 0.0033

19. 32.062 ◯ 32.602

20. 1.0 ◯ 0.1

21. 2 ◯ 2.0

22. 3.6 ◯ 3.5555555

23. 6.42 ◯ 6.24

24. 75.69 ◯ 75.7

25. 4.3 ◯ 4.31

26. 5.2 ◯ 5.02

Reviewing Decimal Operations

Complete this page using pencil and paper. Then use
a calculator to do the same exercises.

Find each sum or difference.

1. $5.5 + 12.87$

2. $34.95 + 4.07$

3. $73 - 8.82$

4. $\$42.34 + \$69.81$

5. $6.72 - 3.543$

6. $4.789 + 5.637$

Find the product.

7. 2.5×4.1

8. 5.006×63

9. 2.36×0.71

10. 5.007×1.3

11. 7.16×0.35

12. 0.23×2.8

Choosing Estimation Techniques

Estimate. Use clustering.

1. 34 + 37 + 36 + 33 _____

2. 9.7 + 10.5 + 10.3 + 9.6 _____

3. 406 + 398 + 410 + 388 _____

4. 58 + 62 + 61 + 59 _____

5. 4.67 + 5.12 + 5.002 + 4.91 _____

6. 21.39 + 18.37 + 20.78 _____

7. 241.3 + 238.8 + 239.5 _____

8. 172.66 + 167.34 + 169.45 _____

9. 508.43 + 489.24 + 502.68 + 497.71

10. 67.8 + 72.7 + 68.3 + 66.9 + 74.5

_____

_____

Estimate. Use front-end estimation and adjust.

11. 68 + 82 + 31 _____

12. 219 + 823 + 605 _____

13. 631 + 228 + 732 + 890 + 543 _____

14. 7.12 + 8.98 + 4.32 + 2.89 _____

15. 27 + 73 + 61 + 59 + 42 _____

16. 34.1 + 59.7 + 68.9 + 81.2 _____

17. 3.06 + 7.23 + 6.78 + 2.12 _____

18. 42.8 + 74.2 + 23.7 + 91.7 _____

19. 12.56 + 28.5 + 41.5 + 59.8 + 60.3

20. 378.5 + 212.9 + 539.4 _____

_____

Estimate. Choose your own method.

21. 5.78 + 6.12 + 5.85 + 6.23 _____

22. 23.7 + 45.1 + 65.9 _____

23. 12.123 + 11.987 + 11.548 _____

24. 124.5 + 126.9 + 125.8 + 124.3 _____

25. 43.7 + 69.2 + 21.8 + 70.9 _____

26. 41.33 + 63.21 + 58.99 + 32.09 _____

27. 2.189 + 2.233 + 2.177 + 2.276 _____

28. 123.4 + 324.9 + 637.8 + 558.6 _____

29. 25.56 + 24.68 + 26.43 + 24.76 _____

30. 3.189 + 3.345 + 3.278 + 3.169 _____

Dividing Decimals

Find the quotients. Round to the nearest tenth.

1. $0.8\overline{)4.3}$ **2.** $0.3\overline{)1.4}$ **3.** $2.7\overline{)12.53}$ **4.** $3.2\overline{)0.49}$

Find the quotients. Round to the nearest hundredth.

5. $6.3\overline{)19.21}$ **6.** $0.25\overline{)0.104}$ **7.** $0.74\overline{)1.293}$

Find the quotients. Round to the nearest thousandth.

8. $0.43\overline{)0.006}$ **9.** $3.8\overline{)2.44}$ **10.** $10.3\overline{)2.6219}$

Problem Solving: Understand the Question

Read each problem. Write a question to complete
the problem.

1. The Andes Mountains in South America are about
   8,850 kilometers long. They are 320 kilometers
   wide except in Bolivia, where they are almost twice
   as wide.

   _____

2. 600 million years ago, the Andes Mountain area
   was a seabed. About 375 million years after that,
   thick layers of sandstone developed and movements
   within the earth folded and lifted the formations
   above the sea. About 70 million years ago, running
   water altered the folds greatly.

   _____

   _____

Read the problem below. Ask yourself the question
in a different way, then solve.

3. The height of a mountain refers to its height above
   sea level. The Himalayan mountain system rises
   from the plains of northern India. These plains have
   an elevation of about 300 meters above sea level.
   Mount Everest, a part of the Himalayas, is 8,848
   meters high. How much higher is Mount Everest
   than the plains of northern India?

   _____

   _____

Exponents and Scientific Notation

Give the missing exponents.

1. $2 \times 2 \times 2 = 2^{\square}$

2. $9 \times 9 \times 9 \times 9 = 9^{\square}$

3. $4 = 4^{\square}$

4. $7 \times 7 = 7^{\square}$

5. $10 \times 10 = 10^{\square}$

6. $3 \times 3 \times 3 \times 3 \times 3 = 3^{\square}$

7. $1 \times 1 \times 1 \times 1 \times 1 \times 1 = 1^{\square}$

8. $6 \times 6 \times 6 = 6^{\square}$

9. $8 \times 8 = 8^{\square}$

10. $5 = 5^{\square}$

11. $5,000 = 5.0 \times 10^{\square}$

12. $32,600 = 3.26 \times 10^{\square}$

13. $2,400,000 = 2.4 \times 10^{\square}$

14. $515,500 = 5.155 \times 10^{\square}$

15. $15,713,000 = 1.5713 \times 10^{\square}$

16. $82,000 = 8.2 \times 10^{\square}$

Complete the table.

	Repeated Factors	Short Form
17.	3×3	
18.		6^4
19.		5^3
20.	$9 \times 9 \times 9 \times 9 \times 9 \times 9$	
21.	8	
22.	$10 \times 10 \times 10 \times 10$	
23.		7^2
24.		10^2

Name _____

Exploring Algebra: Understanding Variables

Use the blocks to help you complete the table to show
how the variables are related.

1.

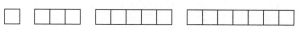

area (*a*)	1	3	5	7	9	11
perimeter (*p*)	4	8	12			

2.

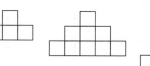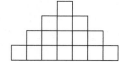

area (*a*)	1	4	9	16	25	36
perimeter (*p*)	4	10	16			

Complete the tables to show how the variables are
related.

3.

tables (*t*)	1	2	3	4	5	9
chairs (*c*)	6	12	18			

4.

cars (*c*)	1	2	3	4	5	6
tires (*t*)	4	8	12			

5.

keys (*k*)	3	6	9	12	15	18
key rings (*r*)	2	4	6			

6.

readers (*r*)	1	2	3	4	5	6
books (*b*)	3	5	7			

7.

cats (*c*)	1	2	3	4	9	15
kittens (*k*)	7	8	9			

8.

spiders (*s*)	1	2	3	4	5
legs (*l*)	8	16	24		

9.

weeks (*w*)	1	2	3	4	5	6
savings (*s*)	$7	$12	$17			

10.

students (*s*)	25	50	75	100	125
classes (*c*)	1	2	3		

11.

radios (*r*)	1	2	3	4	5	10
batteries (*b*)	5	10	15			

12.

muffins (*m*)	12	24	36	48	60
pans (*p*)	1	2	3		

Analyzing Decimal Patterns

Use your knowledge of repeating decimal patterns to decide what two numbers you could divide to obtain the given decimal.

1. $0.878787\ldots =$ _____

2. $0.343434\ldots =$ _____

3. $0.482482\ldots =$ _____

4. $0.555555\ldots =$ _____

5. $0.135135\ldots =$ _____

6. $0.898989\ldots =$ _____

7. $0.020202\ldots =$ _____

8. $0.645645\ldots =$ _____

9. $0.375375\ldots =$ _____

10. $0.070707\ldots =$ _____

Use your knowledge of repeating decimal patterns to decide what decimal will result when you divide these numbers.

11. $7 \div 9 =$ _____

12. $83 \div 99 =$ _____

13. $345 \div 999 =$ _____

14. $869 \div 999 =$ _____

15. $2 \div 9 =$ _____

16. $16 \div 99 =$ _____

Metric Units of Length

Find the missing lengths.

1. 8.5 dm = _____ cm

2. 386 cm = _____ m

3. 16 m = _____ mm

4. 5.91 cm = _____ dm

5. 38.2 m = _____ dm

6. 0.43 m = _____ km

7. 193 dm = _____ m

8. 0.36 m = _____ cm

9. 62 mm = _____ m

10. 168 mm = _____ dm

11. 24.7 km = _____ m

12. 0.5 cm = _____ mm

13. 55 mm = _____ cm

14. 1.7 mm = _____ cm

15. 0.78 m = _____ cm

16. 15,000 m = _____ km

17. 3.5 dam = _____ m

18. 6,000 m = _____ km

19. 461 m = _____ hm

20. 580 dam = _____ km

21. 86 hm = _____ km

22. 51 hm = _____ m

Ring the unit of length that gives the best estimate.

23. The distance from the earth to the moon is about

384,365 _____ .   mm   km   dam

24. A person might be 2 _____ tall.   m   km   hm

25. A honeybee is about 1.5 _____ long.   m   mm   cm

26. A football field is about 50 _____ wide.   dm   km   m

27. A flea is about 3 _____ long.   mm   km   m

Precision in Measurement

In each problem, ring the measurement that is more precise.

1. 68.6 cm to the nearest mm   5 m to the nearest m

2. 413.8 cm to the nearest mm   83.95 km to the nearest dam

3. 2.45 km to the nearest dam   6,000 m to the nearest m

4. 456 km to the nearest km   4,810 m to the nearest m

5. 58.6 km to the nearest hm   692.18 km to the nearest dam

6. 43 dm to the nearest dm   16 mm to the nearest mm

7. 92.36 m to the nearest cm   54.035 m to the nearest mm

8. 3 mm to the nearest mm   3 dam to the nearest dam

9. 18.1 cm to the nearest mm   15.4 m to the nearest dm

10. 76.01 m to the nearest cm   76 m to the nearest m

Give the greatest possible error (GPE) of each measurement.

11. 25 cm _____   12. 83 km _____

13. 17 mm _____   14. 6 dm _____

15. 98 m _____   16. 142 dam _____

17. 5,085 km _____   18. 9 dm _____

19. 62 hm _____   20. 99 cm _____

Mass and Capacity

Complete the following statements.

1. 1 mg = _____ g

2. 1 mL = _____ L

3. 1,000 mg = _____ g

4. 1,000 mL = _____ L

5. 1 g = _____ kg

6. 1 L = _____ kL

7. 1,000 g = _____ kg

8. 1,000 L = _____ kL

9. 6 kg = _____ g

10. 320 kL = _____ L

11. 18 L = _____ mL

12. 2.5 g = _____ mg

13. 450 g = _____ kg

14. 120 L = _____ mL

15. 6 kL = _____ L

16. 94 kg = _____ g

17. 0.33 g = _____ mg

18. 1,500 g = _____ kg

19. 5 mL = _____ L

20. 300 L = _____ kL

Write =, <, or > to complete each statement.

21. 350 mL _____ 1 L

22. 9.5 kg _____ 950 g

23. 225 g _____ 0.225 kg

24. 0.08 kL _____ 0.6 L

25. 0.5 L _____ 3,156 mL

26. 2,400 mg _____ 2.4 g

27. 3 L _____ 3,000 mL

28. 14 g _____ 0.014 kg

29. 1.5 kg _____ 150 g

30. 8.4 L _____ 8,000 mL

Using the Strategies

Use objects or draw a picture to solve the problems below.

1. A car radiator holds 14 quarts of a water-antifreeze mixture. The radiator has a leak and loses 2 quarts of liquid per week. Only 1 quart is replaced each week. How many weeks will it take for the radiator to contain only 1 quart of liquid?

_____

2. There were 18 times as many correct answers as incorrect answers on Kyle's test. If there were 76 items on the test, how many incorrect responses were there?

_____

3. Kate and her brother ride to the movie theater. They pass a roadside fruit stand 2/3 of the way. If the theater is 6 miles from home, how far do they travel after reaching the stand?

_____

4. Anita cut a super sub sandwich into 8 pieces. If she made only parallel cuts, how many slices did she make?

_____

5. Thirty-one bicycles were packed in crates. There were fewer than 6 crates. All crates contained the same number of bicycles except for 1 crate, which held 1 bicycle less than the others. How many crates were there?

_____

How many bicycles were in each crate?

_____

6. A rectangular garden is 4 meters long and 320 centimeters wide. Draw and label a picture of the garden using only centimeter measures. How much greater is the length than the width?

_____

7. Thomas has 3 times as many cassette tapes as Tamara, who has 1/2 as many tapes as Curtis. If Curtis has 10 tapes, how many does Thomas have?

_____

8. Louise makes a display of 28 cereal boxes in the shape of a pyramid, each row having one box fewer than the row below it. If there was 1 box in the top row, how many rows were there?

_____

Multiple Line Graphs

This multiple line graph shows the populations of Rhode Island, Montana, Delaware, and Nevada from 1940 through 1980. Use the graph to answer the questions below.

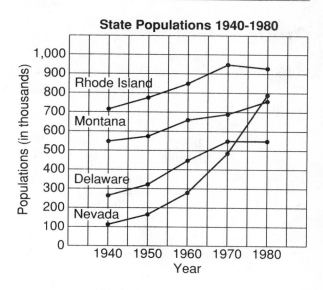

State Populations 1940-1980

Populations (in thousands)

Rhode Island
Montana
Delaware
Nevada

1940 1950 1960 1970 1980
Year

1. Which state had the smallest population?

in 1940? _____

in 1950? _____

in 1960? _____

in 1970? _____

in 1980? _____

2. Which state's population decreased between 1970 and 1980?

_____

3. Which state had the smallest increase in population between 1960 and 1970?

_____

4. Which state had the largest increase in population between 1960 and 1980?

_____

5. The population of Nevada surpassed the population of Delaware during the decade between

_____ and _____ .

6. Estimate the difference between the population of Nevada and Rhode Island

in 1940 _____

in 1960 _____

in 1980 _____

Is this difference increasing or decreasing?

_____

Circle Graphs

The circle graph at the right shows how the annual budget for the drama club is spent. Examine the graph and answer the questions.

1. Is more or less than half of the budget spent on costumes and props?

_____

2. How much is spent on equipment rental?

_____

3. How much is spent on refreshments?

_____

Drama Club Budget
$3,000

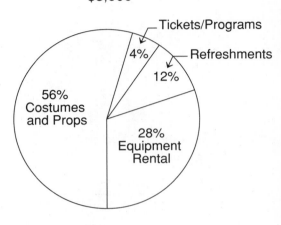

4. How much more is spent on refreshments than on tickets and programs?

_____

5. If the budget is increased 10% next year, about how much could be spent on costumes and props?

_____

What is wrong with this circle graph?

6. _____

_____

_____

Athletic Club Budget
$5,000

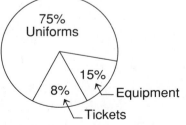

7. _____

_____

Scattergrams

Examine the table. Using these data, construct a
scattergram, then write answers to the exercises that
follow.

Minutes of piano practice per week	350	250	275	75	325	175	150
Score in district music jamboree	98%	90%	93%	70%	95%	85%	80%

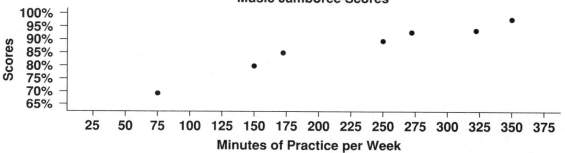

1. Is there a positive correlation between weekly
practice time and District Music Jamboree

scores? Explain. _____

_____

2. Suppose a pianist has the talent, experience, and
quality of instruction equal to those who entered the
music jamboree. What score would you predict if

this pianist practiced 300 minutes per week? _____

Do you feel that a graph can be a good predictor

of music contest scores? _____

Why or why not? _____

_____

_____

Choosing Mental Math Techniques

Solve using mental math. Use compensation.

1. $50 + 798 =$ _____

2. $258 - 29 =$ _____

3. $45 + 355 =$ _____

4. $8 \times 42 =$ _____

5. $351 - 12 =$ _____

6. $49 \times 6 =$ _____

7. $47 + 699 =$ _____

8. $3 \times 28 =$ _____

9. $500 - 98 =$ _____

Solve using mental math. Use the break apart technique.

10. $11 \times 823 =$ _____

11. $721 - 19 =$ _____

12. $65 + 95 =$ _____

13. $8 \times 24 =$ _____

14. $140 - 7 =$ _____

15. $709 - 12 =$ _____

16. $518 + 42 =$ _____

17. $63 + 17 =$ _____

18. $73 \times 4 =$ _____

Solve using mental math. Use either compensation or the break apart technique.

19. $18 \times 20 =$ _____

20. $258 + 23 =$ _____

21. $351 - 42 =$ _____

22. $127 - 40 =$ _____

23. $159 + 28 =$ _____

24. $\$4.50 \times 6 =$ _____

25. $14 + 89 =$ _____

26. $15 \times 60 =$ _____

27. $423 - 25 =$ _____

Use mental math to find the missing numbers.

28. $(12 + \underline{\hspace{1.5cm}}) \times 2 = 84$

29. $(25 \times \underline{\hspace{1.5cm}}) - 2 = 148$

30. $100 - (6 \times \underline{\hspace{1.5cm}}) = 52$

31. $77 + (\underline{\hspace{1.5cm}} \times 6) = 101$

32. $(36 + \underline{\hspace{1.5cm}}) - 2 = 68$

33. $(14 + \underline{\hspace{1.5cm}}) \times 3 = 72$

Name _____

Choosing an Appropriate Graph

A bar graph, a line graph, and a circle graph are needed
below. Decide which type of graph is appropriate for
each set of data. Sketch each graph.

1. 4–H members who raised sheep over six years.

4–H Members Raising Sheep

1986	90%
1987	91%
1988	85%
1989	86%
1990	84%
1991	89%

2. The number of sheep raised on an Australian sheep
station over four years.

Sheep Raised

1986	14,900
1987	9,900
1988	24,900
1989	29,900

3. The percentages of a 1990 herd of sheep that were
raised for wool, for meat and to show in fairs.

Uses for Sheep Raised in 1990

Wool	Meat	Show
50%	40%	10%

Using the Strategies

Solve, using Guess and Check or Draw a Picture.

1. Steak costs 3 times as much as chicken. If steak is selling for $3.57 per pound, how much per pound does chicken sell for?

_____

How much does 5 pounds of chicken cost?

_____

2. If Jeni worked 8 more hours washing cars than did Amber, and together they worked a total of 26 hours, how many hours did each girl spend working?

_____

_____

3. Pat positioned a post in each corner of his rectangular yard, put 4 at the gate entrance, and gave 3 to his neighbor. How many does he have left over if he purchased a bundle of 15 posts?

_____

4. Jason has 2 hats, 2 jackets, 3 shirts, and 1 pair of comfortable jeans. How many different outfits can he choose?

_____

5. Alyssa bought 3 shirts at $16.95 each and a $24 sweater. How much change did she receive if she gave the cashier $100?

_____

6. Darren had a balance of $45 in his bank account. He deposited $8 each week for 17 weeks and withdrew $23 twice. How much money is in his account?

_____

Mean, Median, and Mode

Find the mean, median, and mode for each set of
data. Use a calculator.

1. 50	**2.** 6	**3.** 100	**4.** 1.6
20	6	96	1.7
42	8	104	1.8
45	10	103	
48	11	105	
50			

Mean = _____   Mean = _____   Mean = _____   Mean = _____

Median = _____   Median = _____   Median = _____   Median = _____

Mode = _____   Mode = _____   Mode = _____   Mode = _____

5. 6	**6.** 1.6	**7.** 10	**8.** 60
8	1.4	16	60
11	1.0	11	63
10	1.0	17	60
13	0.5	20	

Mean = _____   Mean = _____   Mean = _____   Mean = _____

Median = _____   Median = _____   Median = _____   Median = _____

Mode = _____   Mode = _____   Mode = _____   Mode = _____

Stem-and-Leaf Tables

Daryl's class held a gift exchange. His teacher asked each student to record the price of the gift he or she brought. She placed the data in a stem-and-leaf table. For example, the teacher placed a 2 under the stem and 25 under the leaf to represent $2.25.

Examine the stem-and-leaf table and answer the questions.

Stem	Leaf
2	25, 89, 75, 62, 99, 91, 95
3	50, 25, 15, 89, 95, 99, 97, 99, 50
4	45, 50, 75, 99, 99, 49, 15, 50
5	0, 0, 4

1. Which price range–$2, $3, $4, or $5–was the most common? _____

2. How many students were in Daryl's class? _____

3. How many gifts cost $3.50? _____

4. How many gifts cost more than $3.97? _____

5. How many gifts cost less than $3.97? _____

6. Is $3.97 the mean, median, or mode for this set of data? _____

Why? _____

7. What is the range for the data above? _____

Make a stem-and-leaf table for the following data.

Hourly wages: $7.98, $5.50, $7.25, $6.75, $5.10, $7.50, $6.80, $5.25, $7.15, $6.50, $7.05, $5.85, $7.75, $6.80, $7.50, $5.75, $7.75

Stem	Leaf

Frequency Tables and Histograms

Below are class scores for 29 students on a recent science report. Organize these data on the table.

Scores: 89, 97, 98, 95, 85, 88, 84, 79, 78, 95, 88, 98, 100, 99, 95, 86, 87, 75, 71, 73, 89, 90, 92, 83, 83, 85, 75, 77, 77

Class Science Report Scores		
Scores	Tally	Frequency
70–75	‖‖	
75–80	‖‖	
80–85	‖‖‖	
85–90	‖‖‖ ‖	
90–95	‖‖‖	
95–100	‖‖‖	
		Total _____

Data from a frequency table can be shown on a bar graph called a histogram. The bars should touch.

Using the data above, construct a histogram. Use a ruler.

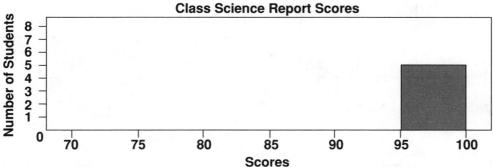

Exploring Algebra: More About Variables

Examine the tables. Discover the relationship between each number in the top row and the number below it. Write a rule that describes this relationship. Complete the tables.

1.

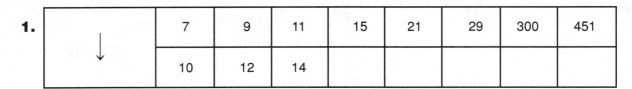

↓	7	9	11	15	21	29	300	451
	10	12	14					

RULE: To find the bottom number _____

_____.

2.

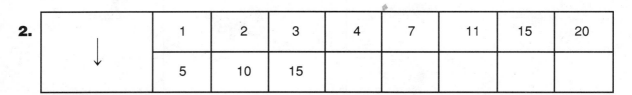

↓	1	2	3	4	7	11	15	20
	5	10	15					

RULE: To find the bottom number _____

_____.

3.

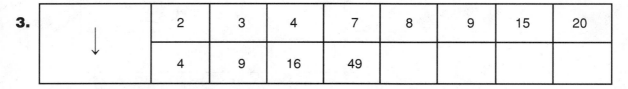

↓	2	3	4	7	8	9	15	20
	4	9	16	49				

RULE: To find the bottom number _____

_____.

4.

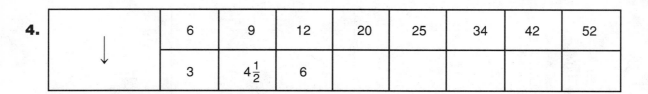

↓	6	9	12	20	25	34	42	52
	3	$4\frac{1}{2}$	6					

RULE: To find the bottom number _____

_____.

Extra Data

Solve each problem and write the unneeded data.

1. A clothing manager paid $12 for each set of 6 handkerchiefs she bought from a wholesale dealer. She sold them in sets of 4 for $10. Of the 234 handkerchiefs she bought, she sold 20. How much profit did she make on the ones she sold?

_____

_____

_____

2. A certain jet is about 71 meters long, has a wingspan of about 60 meters, and seats 3 times as many passengers as a smaller plane. If the length and wing span of future jets are expected to be reduced by 0.5 meter, what will the wingspan of a newer jet probably be?

_____

_____

_____

3. A can filled with varnish weighs 36 pounds. The can itself weighs 2 pounds. A smaller can filled with paint weighs one third that of the varnish-filled can. How much does the smaller paint-filled can weigh?

_____

_____

_____

4. The peel of a particular banana weighs about one eighth the weight of the banana. Bananas cost 47¢ a pound. If you buy 9 pounds of bananas and throw away 1 pound due to spoilage, how much did you spend on bananas?

_____

_____

_____

Exploring Solid Figures

State whether each figure is a prism or a pyramid.
Write the number of vertices (*V*), faces (*F*), and edges
(*E*) of each figure. Verify that $V + F - E = 2$.

1.

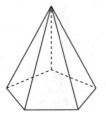

_____

V _____

F _____

E _____

____ + ____ − ____ = 2

2.

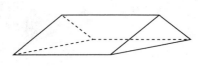

_____

V _____

F _____

E _____

____ + ____ − ____ = 2

3.

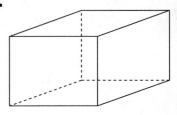

_____

V _____

F _____

E _____

____ + ____ − ____ = 2

4.

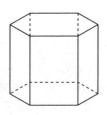

_____

V _____

F _____

E _____

____ + ____ − ____ = 2

5.

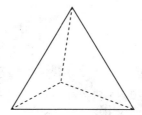

_____

V _____

F _____

E _____

____ + ____ − ____ = 2

6.

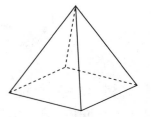

_____

V _____

F _____

E _____

____ + ____ − ____ = 2

Visualizing Cross Sections

Use a ruler. Draw a picture of each cross section.

1.

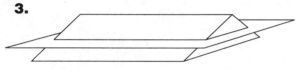

2.

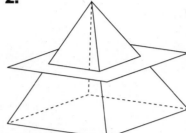

3.

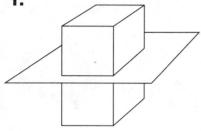

4.

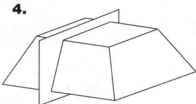

5.

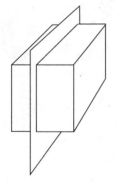

6.

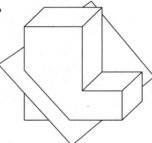

7.

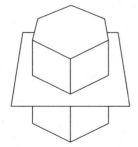

8.

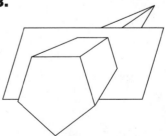

Drawing Plane Figures

Use a ruler and a protractor. Draw and label each
geometric figure.

1. a 50° angle *DEF*

2. a 110° angle *PQR*

3. a 65° angle *XYZ*

4. a triangle whose angles include a
40° angle and a 60° angle

5. a triangle with a 120° angle

6. a quadrilateral whose angles include
a 70° angle and a 100° angle

Find the measure of each angle's complementary angle.

7. 60° _____

8. 18° _____

9. 89° _____

Find the measure of each angle's supplementary angle.

10. 3° _____

11. 122° _____

12. 90° _____

Name _____

Using Critical Thinking Skills

Write a statement for each diagram. Tell whether the
statement is true or false. Explain why.

1. Rhombuses

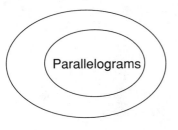

_____

_____

_____

_____

2. Parallelograms

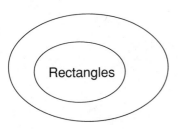

_____

_____

_____

_____

3. Equilateral Triangles

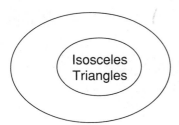

_____

_____

_____

_____

4. Scalene Triangles

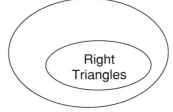

_____

_____

_____

_____

Name _____

Angle Sum Relationships

Find the measure of ∠A in each triangle below.

1.

m ∠ A = _____

2.

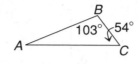

m ∠ A = _____

3.

m ∠ A = _____

4.

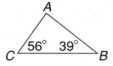

m ∠ A = _____

5.

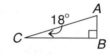

m ∠ A = _____

6.

m ∠ A = _____

Find the measure of ∠ D in each quadrilateral below.

7.

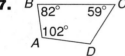

m ∠ D = _____

8.

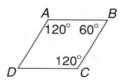

m ∠ D = _____

9.

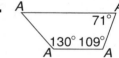

m ∠ D = _____

Answer the questions below.

10. An isosceles triangle has two angles that each measure 40°. What is the measure of the third angle?

_____

11. Find the measure of the third angle of a triangle if the measures of the other two angles are 110° and 38°.

_____

12. Find the measure of the fourth angle of a quadrilateral if the other three measures are 81°, 79°, and 120°.

_____

13. One of the acute angles of a right triangle measures 39°. Find the measure of the other acute angle.

_____

14. An obtuse angle of an isosceles triangle measures 110°. Find the measure of one of the acute angles.

_____

Exploring Algebra: Understanding Equations

Make an equation by supplying the missing number.

1. $\boxed{} - 75 = 25$ **2.** $\boxed{} + 39 = 81$ **3.** $\boxed{} + 115 = 119$

4. $99 - \boxed{} = 44$ **5.** $\boxed{} - 49 = 59$ **6.** $72 + \boxed{} = 72$

7. $7 \times \boxed{} = 7$ **8.** $\boxed{} \div 15 = 6$ **9.** $11 \times \boxed{} = 110$

10. $\boxed{} \div 3 = 23$ **11.** $\boxed{} \div 100 = 1$ **12.** $5 \times \boxed{} = 325$

Use a calculator to help decide if each example is
an equation. Use <, >, or = to make the statement
true.

13. $81{,}000 \div 90 \bigcirc 9{,}000$ **14.** $45.11 \times 0.35 \bigcirc 157{,}885$

15. $367.17 \times 100 \bigcirc 36{,}717$ **16.** $54.081 \div 0.9 \bigcirc 6.009$

17. $3.6 \div 4 \bigcirc 0.9$ **18.** $28.064 \div 0.04 \bigcirc 710.6$

19. $457 \times 90 \bigcirc 4{,}113$ **20.** $112 \times 17 \bigcirc 1{,}904$

21. $60 \times 70 \bigcirc 420$ **22.** $110 \times 30 \bigcirc 3{,}300$

23. $27{,}373 \div 100 \bigcirc 273.73$ **24.** $39{,}009 \div 100 \bigcirc 390.09$

25. $105.2 \div 10 \bigcirc 10.52$ **26.** $440 + 660 \bigcirc 1{,}000$

27. $1{,}999 + 101 \bigcirc 2{,}100$ **28.** $0.7 \times 7.03 \bigcirc 4.95$

Using the Strategies

Use the strategy Guess and Check or Make an Organized List to solve each problem.

1. Jonathan has 2 more dimes than nickels. If the total value is $0.95, how many dimes does he have?

_____

How many nickels? _____

2. The first angle of a triangle is twice as large as its second angle. The third angle is 3 times as large as the second angle. The sum of the measures of a triangle is 180°. What are the measures of the angles?

_____ _____ _____

3. The sum of the lengths of the sides of a triangle is 31 cm. There are 2 congruent sides, each of which is 5 cm longer than the third side. Find the length of each side.

_____

4. The game Trivial Endeavors has 5-point questions and 4-point questions. Karla scored 30 points on her 7 correctly answered questions. How many 4 point questions did she answer correctly?

_____

5. Current event teams consist of 2 or 3 members. A class of 28 students was divided into 11 current event teams. How many groups of 2 were there?

_____

How many groups of 3?

_____

6. The library charges $0.25 for the first day a book is overdue and $0.05 for each day after that. Angela paid a total of $1.10 in fines for 2 books checked out together and returned the same day. How many days overdue was each book?

_____

Parallel and Perpendicular Lines

1. Name a pair of parallel lines. _____

2. Name a transversal. _____

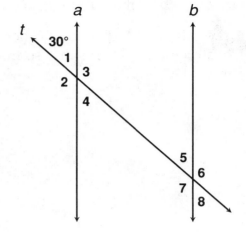

3. Find: m ∠ 2 = _____   m ∠ 3 = _____

    m ∠ 4 = _____   m ∠ 5 = _____

    m ∠ 6 = _____   m ∠ 7 = _____

    m ∠ 8 = _____

4. Name a pair of parallel lines. _____

5. Name a transversal. _____

6. Find: m ∠ 1 = _____   m ∠ 2 = _____

    m ∠ 3 = _____   m ∠ 4 = _____

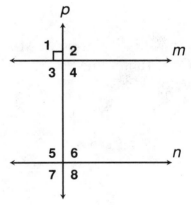

7. ∠1, ∠2, ∠3, and ∠4 are all angles with measures

    of _____

8. p _____ m

9. m ∠ 5 = _____   m ∠ 6 = _____

    m ∠ 7 = _____   m ∠ 8 = _____

10. ∠5, ∠6, ∠7, and ∠8 are all angles with measures

    of _____

11. p _____ n

Constructing Parallel and Perpendicular Lines

Construct each of the following.

1. Draw a line *l*. Mark a point *S* not on *l*. Construct a line *t* through *S* so that *t* ⊥ *l*.

2. Draw a line *n*. Mark a point *T* on *n*. Construct a line *w* through *T* so that *w* ⊥ *n*.

3. Draw line *f* and point M not on *f*. Construct a line *j* so that *j* || *f* through point *M*.

4. Construct three parallel lines so that the middle line is halfway between the other two.

Constructing Angle and Segment Bisectors

Complete the following constructions. Verify that the
bisections are correct with a ruler and a protractor.

1. Draw an acute angle. Construct its angle bisector.

What is the measure of the original angle? _____

What is the measure of each of the two new angles? _____ and _____

2. Draw an angle that has a measure of 140°. Construct its angle bisector.

What is the measure of each of the two new angles? _____ and _____

A ray that bisects an obtuse angle will always form two _____ angles.

3. Draw a line segment that is 5 inches long. Construct its perpendicular bisector.

What is the measure of each of the two new segments? _____ and _____

Constructing Triangles

Use a compass and a straightedge to do the following constructions.

1. Using $\overline{DE}$, $\overline{EF}$, and $\overline{DF}$, construct $\triangle DEF$.

D————E   E—F   D————————F

2. Construct an equilateral triangle with sides 1.5 in.

3. Construct an isosceles triangle with two sides 2 in.

4. Construct a right triangle with sides 1.5 in., 2 in., and 2.5 in.

Problem Solving: Data from a Chart

Cities	Driving Time (h)
Johnstown to Owensville	1.5
Owensville to Fleming	0.75
Fleming to Cypress	0.5
Cypress to Johnstown	1.6
Johnstown to Fleming	2.2
Owensville to Cypress	1.2

Use the chart data to solve these problems.

1. Rose drove from Owensville to Fleming and then from Fleming to Cypress. What was her driving time?

_____

2. There is a fruit stand $\frac{1}{2}$ of the way between Fleming and Cypress. How long does it take to get to the fruit stand from Fleming.

_____

3. How much longer does it take to drive from Johnstown to Owensville than it takes to drive from Owensville to Cypress?

_____

4. Oscar and Mandy are going to share driving from Cypress to Johnstown. How long should each person drive?

_____

5. How much longer does it take to drive from Johnstown to Owensville to Fleming than to drive directly from Johnstown to Fleming?

_____

6. Alice drove from Cypress to Johnstown and then returned to Cypress. What was her driving time?

_____

7. Bill is on his way to Cypress from Owensville. He has driven 0.8h. How much longer must he drive to get to Cypress?

_____

8. Frank drove from Cypress to Johnstown and from Johnstown to Fleming. What was his driving time?

_____

Divisibility

Ring the numbers that are divisible by 3.

1. 48   **2.** 75   **3.** 76   **4.** 77   **5.** 78

6. 761   **7.** 762   **8.** 763   **9.** 764   **10.** 765

Ring the numbers that are divisible by 4.

11. 934   **12.** 924   **13.** 944   **14.** 954   **15.** 964

16. 732   **17.** 742   **18.** 752   **18.** 762   **20.** 772

Ring the numbers that are divisible by 6.

21. 36   **22.** 54   **23.** 79   **24.** 90   **25.** 241

26. 324   **27.** 243   **28.** 432   **29.** 423   **30.** 234

Ring the numbers that are divisible by 8.

31. 354   **32.** 352   **33.** 376   **34.** 384   **35.** 392

36. 648   **37.** 608   **38.** 506   **39.** 560   **40.** 1,055

Ring the numbers that are divisible by 9.

41. 377   **42.** 378   **43.** 387   **44.** 837   **45.** 827

46. 4,876   **47.** 5,876   **48.** 5,976   **49.** 9,567   **50.** 5,796

Factors, Primes, and Composites

List all of the factors of each number.

1. 57 _____   **2.** 64 _____

3. 19 _____   **4.** 16 _____

5. 28 _____   **6.** 97 _____

7. 75 _____   **8.** 44 _____

Identify each number as prime or composite.

9. 91 _____   **10.** 59 _____   **11.** 87 _____

12. 89 _____   **13.** 51 _____   **14.** 49 _____

15. 7 _____   **16.** 46 _____   **17.** 37 _____

Express each of the following odd numbers as the sum
of 3 prime numbers.

18. 21 _____   **19.** 29 _____

20. 83 _____   **21.** 55 _____

22. 31 _____   **23.** 47 _____

24. 53 _____   **25.** 99 _____

Prime Factorization

Complete each factor tree. Write the prime factorization of each number.

1.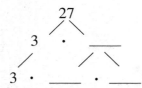

27 = _____

2.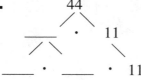

44 = _____

3.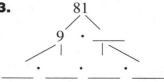

81 = _____

4.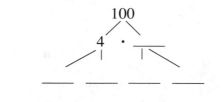

100 = _____

5.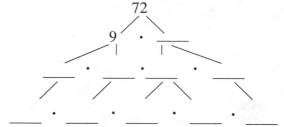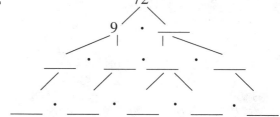

72 = _____

Write the prime factorization of each number using exponents.

6. 9 _____

7. 10 _____

8. 12 _____

9. 18 _____

10. 24 _____

11. 28 _____

12. 36 _____

13. 48 _____

14. 54 _____

15. 60 _____

16. 88 _____

17. 91 _____

18. 96 _____

19. 104 _____

20. 120 _____

21. 125 _____

Name _____

Greatest Common Factor

1. List the factors of 12. _____

2. List the factors of 30. _____

3. List the common factors of 12 and 30. _____

4. What is the greatest common factor (GCF) of 12 and 30? _____

Find the GCF of each pair of numbers.

5. $60 = 2 \cdot 2 \cdot 3 \cdot 5$

  $75 = 3 \cdot 5 \cdot 5$ _____

6. $40 = 2 \cdot 2 \cdot 2 \cdot 5$

  $90 = 2 \cdot 3 \cdot 3 \cdot 5$ _____

7. $45 = 3 \cdot 3 \cdot 5$

  $120 = 2 \cdot 2 \cdot 2 \cdot 3 \cdot 5$ _____

8. $54 = 2 \cdot 3 \cdot 3 \cdot 3$

  $72 = 2 \cdot 2 \cdot 2 \cdot 3 \cdot 3$ _____

9. $42 = 2 \cdot 3 \cdot 7$

  $63 = 3 \cdot 3 \cdot 7$ _____

10. $70 = 2 \cdot 5 \cdot 7$

  $105 = 3 \cdot 5 \cdot 7$ _____

Find the GCF of each pair of numbers.

11. 4 and 14 _____

12. 24 and 54 _____

13. 12 and 28 _____

14. 45 and 42 _____

15. 15 and 24 _____

16. 48 and 60 _____

17. 20 and 32 _____

18. 80 and 128 _____

19. 21 and 25 _____

20. 48 and 200 _____

Least Common Multiple

Use prime factorization to find the least common multiple (LCM) of each pair of numbers.

1. 14 _____

    21 _____

    LCM _____

2. 9 _____

    12 _____

    LCM _____

3. 24 _____

    18 _____

    LCM _____

4. 15 _____

    20 _____

    LCM _____

5. 10 _____

    12 _____

    LCM _____

6. 4 _____

    6 _____

    LCM _____

List multiples to find the LCM of each pair of numbers.

7. 20 _____

    24 _____

    LCM _____

8. 18 _____

    48 _____

    LCM _____

9. 12 _____

    15 _____

    LCM _____

10. 30 _____

    12 _____

    LCM _____

11. 16 _____

    32 _____

    LCM _____

12. 8 _____

    14 _____

    LCM _____

Write the LCM of each pair of numbers.

13. 4, 10 _____

14. 8, 12 _____

15. 6, 15 _____

16. 16, 20 _____

17. 8, 30 _____

18. 8, 9 _____

19. 10, 15 _____

20. 24, 30 _____

Discovering Prime Number Patterns

Create an ordered list of prime numbers between 1 and 100.
Verify that they are prime by applying divisibility rules.

HINT: You should find 25 prime numbers.

_____

_____

Identify pairs of twin primes.
Write the sum of each pair below.
Which number belongs to two pairs? _____

1. _____   **2.** _____   **3.** _____

4. _____   **5.** _____   **6.** _____

7. _____   **8.** _____

Equivalent Fractions

Find the missing numerator or denominator.

1. $\dfrac{1}{2} = \dfrac{}{8}$

2. $\dfrac{3}{4} = \dfrac{12}{}$

3. $\dfrac{2}{5} = \dfrac{}{15}$

4. $\dfrac{5}{7} = \dfrac{20}{}$

5. $\dfrac{4}{9} = \dfrac{}{36}$

6. $\dfrac{5}{6} = \dfrac{25}{}$

7. $\dfrac{4}{3} = \dfrac{}{18}$

8. $\dfrac{7}{8} = \dfrac{35}{}$

9. $\dfrac{3}{10} = \dfrac{}{50}$

10. $\dfrac{11}{12} = \dfrac{33}{}$

11. $\dfrac{1}{4} = \dfrac{}{40}$

12. $\dfrac{5}{12} = \dfrac{}{48}$

13. $\dfrac{3}{5} = \dfrac{24}{}$

14. $\dfrac{1}{3} = \dfrac{}{12}$

15. $\dfrac{5}{16} = \dfrac{}{32}$

16. $\dfrac{1}{6} = \dfrac{6}{}$

17. $\dfrac{5}{8} = \dfrac{}{64}$

18. $\dfrac{7}{10} = \dfrac{70}{}$

19. $\dfrac{13}{20} = \dfrac{}{100}$

20. $\dfrac{5}{9} = \dfrac{}{45}$

Write the next three equivalent fractions.

21. $\dfrac{1}{2}, \dfrac{2}{4}, \dfrac{3}{6},$ _____ , _____ , _____

22. $\dfrac{2}{5}, \dfrac{4}{10}, \dfrac{6}{15},$ _____ , _____ , _____

23. $\dfrac{4}{7}, \dfrac{8}{14}, \dfrac{12}{21},$ _____ , _____ , _____

24. $\dfrac{3}{4}, \dfrac{6}{8}, \dfrac{9}{12},$ _____ , _____ , _____

25. $\dfrac{5}{6}, \dfrac{10}{12}, \dfrac{15}{18},$ _____ , _____ , _____

26. $\dfrac{9}{11}, \dfrac{18}{22}, \dfrac{27}{33},$ _____ , _____ , _____

Write an equivalent fraction with a denominator of 20 for each fraction.

27. $\dfrac{3}{10} =$ _____

28. $\dfrac{1}{2} =$ _____

29. $\dfrac{3}{4} =$ _____

30. $\dfrac{2}{5} =$ _____

Write an equivalent fraction with a denominator of 100 for each fraction.

31. $\dfrac{3}{50} =$ _____

32. $\dfrac{1}{2} =$ _____

33. $\dfrac{7}{25} =$ _____

34. $\dfrac{1}{5} =$ _____

Lowest Terms

Give the GCF of the numerator and denominator.

1. $\dfrac{15}{20}$ _____

2. $\dfrac{18}{25}$ _____

3. $\dfrac{90}{100}$ _____

4. $\dfrac{25}{75}$ _____

5. $\dfrac{24}{30}$ _____

6. $\dfrac{21}{30}$ _____

7. $\dfrac{55}{88}$ _____

8. $\dfrac{21}{700}$ _____

9. $\dfrac{25}{40}$ _____

10. $\dfrac{27}{54}$ _____

11. $\dfrac{36}{90}$ _____

12. $\dfrac{72}{90}$ _____

Write each fraction in lowest terms.

13. $\dfrac{6}{15} =$ _____

14. $\dfrac{12}{27} =$ _____

15. $\dfrac{15}{40} =$ _____

16. $\dfrac{42}{48} =$ _____

17. $\dfrac{6}{60} =$ _____

18. $\dfrac{18}{30} =$ _____

19. $\dfrac{8}{12} =$ _____

20. $\dfrac{13}{52} =$ _____

21. $\dfrac{24}{42} =$ _____

22. $\dfrac{50}{75} =$ _____

23. $\dfrac{14}{20} =$ _____

24. $\dfrac{16}{40} =$ _____

25. $\dfrac{34}{50} =$ _____

26. $\dfrac{40}{70} =$ _____

27. $\dfrac{7}{28} =$ _____

28. $\dfrac{16}{30} =$ _____

29. $\dfrac{40}{100} =$ _____

30. $\dfrac{9}{24} =$ _____

31. $\dfrac{21}{35} =$ _____

32. $\dfrac{8}{20} =$ _____

33. $\dfrac{4}{16} =$ _____

34. $\dfrac{3}{18} =$ _____

35. $\dfrac{9}{36} =$ _____

36. $\dfrac{12}{24} =$ _____

Improper Fractions and Mixed Numbers

Write each improper fraction as a mixed number or a whole number.

1. $\frac{11}{8}$ _____

2. $\frac{23}{2}$ _____

3. $\frac{25}{10}$ _____

4. $\frac{33}{4}$ _____

5. $\frac{15}{4}$ _____

6. $\frac{13}{10}$ _____

7. $\frac{43}{8}$ _____

8. $\frac{280}{100}$ _____

9. $\frac{18}{5}$ _____

10. $\frac{20}{4}$ _____

11. $\frac{65}{7}$ _____

12. $\frac{1,500}{600}$ _____

13. $\frac{36}{5}$ _____

14. $\frac{83}{8}$ _____

15. $\frac{123}{10}$ _____

16. $\frac{57}{8}$ _____

17. $\frac{76}{3}$ _____

18. $\frac{33}{8}$ _____

19. $\frac{56}{8}$ _____

20. $\frac{97}{5}$ _____

21. $\frac{25}{6}$ _____

22. $\frac{100}{3}$ _____

23. $\frac{75}{2}$ _____

24. $\frac{258}{6}$ _____

Write each mixed number as an improper fraction.

25. $1\frac{1}{8}$ _____

26. $6\frac{2}{3}$ _____

27. $8\frac{3}{4}$ _____

28. $23\frac{7}{10}$ _____

29. $3\frac{1}{5}$ _____

30. $23\frac{1}{2}$ _____

31. $12\frac{1}{3}$ _____

32. $5\frac{19}{100}$ _____

33. $5\frac{9}{10}$ _____

34. $15\frac{1}{4}$ _____

35. $8\frac{4}{5}$ _____

36. $3\frac{7}{1,000}$ _____

37. $9\frac{7}{8}$ _____

38. $10\frac{3}{4}$ _____

39. $6\frac{3}{10}$ _____

40. $12\frac{1}{4}$ _____

41. $16\frac{2}{3}$ _____

42. $1\frac{9}{10}$ _____

43. $10\frac{4}{5}$ _____

44. $3\frac{7}{100}$ _____

45. $18\frac{1}{3}$ _____

46. $7\frac{5}{6}$ _____

47. $19\frac{3}{8}$ _____

48. $36\frac{1}{2}$ _____

Name _____

Exploring Algebra: More About Equations

These scales are balanced.
Decide which of the scales
below are also balanced.
Write **balanced** below
those that are.

1.

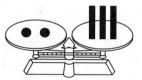

_____

2.

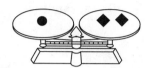

_____

3.

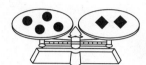

_____

4.

_____

5.

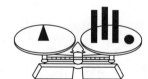

_____

6.

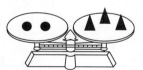

_____

7.

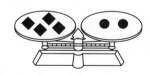

_____

8.

_____

9.

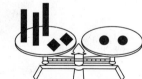

_____

Write an equation for each balanced scale. What shapes will balance ■ ?

10.

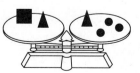

_____

_____

11.

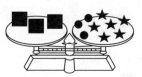

_____

_____

Fractions and Decimals

Write as a decimal and as a lowest-terms fraction or mixed number.

1. 4 tenths

_____

2. 17 hundredths

_____

3. 1 and 7 tenths

_____

4. 30 hundredths

_____

5. 750 thousandths

_____

6. 5 and 20 hundredths

_____

7. 25 thousandths

_____

8. 6 and 5 tenths

_____

9. 500 ten thousandths

_____

Write each decimal as a lowest-terms fraction or mixed number.

10. 0.2 _____

11. 0.28 _____

12. 0.05 _____

13. 0.3 _____

14. 0.06 _____

15. 4.75 _____

16. 9.8 _____

17. 0.625 _____

18. 0.45 _____

19. 3.15 _____

20. 7.6 _____

21. 0.004 _____

Write each fraction as a decimal.

22. $\frac{3}{4}$ _____

23. $\frac{6}{10}$ _____

24. $2\frac{1}{4}$ _____

25. $\frac{2}{5}$ _____

26. $\frac{9}{20}$ _____

27. $1\frac{4}{10}$ _____

28. $\frac{17}{25}$ _____

29. $\frac{46}{100}$ _____

30. $\frac{22}{50}$ _____

31. $6\frac{1}{5}$ _____

32. $\frac{418}{1,000}$ _____

33. $3\frac{89}{100}$ _____

Name _____

Terminating and Repeating Decimals

Write each repeating decimal using a bar.

1. 4.166666…

_____

2. 0.515151…

_____

3. 6.243243…

_____

4.

0.062062…

_____

5. 1.259259…

_____

6. 0.133333…

_____

With a calculator, find the decimal for each fraction.
Use a bar to show repeating decimals.

7. $\frac{4}{9}$ _____

8. $\frac{3}{25}$ _____

9. $\frac{4}{3}$ _____

10. $\frac{1}{6}$ _____

11. $\frac{19}{15}$ _____

12. $\frac{7}{5}$ _____

13. $\frac{5}{27}$ _____

14. $\frac{1}{18}$ _____

15. $\frac{11}{20}$ _____

With a calculator, discover the pattern and complete each row.
Use a bar to show repeating decimals.

16. $\frac{1}{15}$, $0.1\overline{3}$, $\frac{1}{5}$, _____, _____, _____, _____, _____, $\frac{3}{5}$

17. 0.25, 1.5, 2.75, _____, _____, _____, _____, _____, 10.25

18. $\frac{1}{18}$, $0.1\overline{6}$, $\frac{5}{18}$, _____, _____, _____, _____, _____, $\frac{17}{18}$

Comparing and Ordering Fractions

Compare the fractions. Write $>$ or $<$ for each $\bigcirc$.

1. $\dfrac{3}{5} \bigcirc \dfrac{3}{4}$ **2.** $\dfrac{4}{15} \bigcirc \dfrac{3}{10}$ **3.** $\dfrac{3}{8} \bigcirc \dfrac{5}{12}$ **4.** $\dfrac{7}{12} \bigcirc \dfrac{2}{3}$

5. $\dfrac{2}{3} \bigcirc \dfrac{3}{5}$ **6.** $\dfrac{2}{5} \bigcirc \dfrac{3}{10}$ **7.** $\dfrac{7}{8} \bigcirc \dfrac{9}{10}$ **8.** $\dfrac{5}{10} \bigcirc \dfrac{52}{100}$

9. $\dfrac{2}{3} \bigcirc \dfrac{4}{9}$ **10.** $\dfrac{1}{6} \bigcirc \dfrac{3}{12}$ **11.** $\dfrac{1}{2} \bigcirc \dfrac{3}{5}$ **12.** $\dfrac{3}{10} \bigcirc \dfrac{47}{100}$

13. $\dfrac{13}{22} \bigcirc \dfrac{2}{3}$ **14.** $\dfrac{7}{9} \bigcirc \dfrac{7}{8}$ **15.** $\dfrac{5}{11} \bigcirc \dfrac{19}{40}$ **16.** $\dfrac{13}{18} \bigcirc \dfrac{16}{20}$

Compare the mixed numbers. Write $>$ or $<$ for each $\bigcirc$.

17. $1\dfrac{5}{16} \bigcirc 1\dfrac{3}{8}$ **18.** $2\dfrac{1}{2} \bigcirc 1\dfrac{7}{8}$ **19.** $6\dfrac{7}{9} \bigcirc 6\dfrac{5}{6}$ **20.** $4\dfrac{1}{2} \bigcirc 4\dfrac{3}{7}$

21. $5\dfrac{2}{15} \bigcirc 5\dfrac{1}{5}$ **22.** $3\dfrac{1}{4} \bigcirc 3\dfrac{3}{8}$ **23.** $8\dfrac{5}{11} \bigcirc 8\dfrac{3}{4}$ **24.** $1\dfrac{2}{3} \bigcirc 1\dfrac{5}{8}$

25. $9\dfrac{4}{9} \bigcirc 9\dfrac{6}{10}$ **26.** $7\dfrac{7}{10} \bigcirc 7\dfrac{5}{6}$ **27.** $2\dfrac{5}{7} \bigcirc 2\dfrac{5}{6}$ **28.** $5\dfrac{3}{8} \bigcirc 5\dfrac{1}{2}$

Arrange the fractions or mixed numbers in order from smallest to largest.

29. $\dfrac{5}{6}, \ \dfrac{5}{7}, \ \dfrac{3}{4}, \ \dfrac{2}{3}, \ \dfrac{9}{11}, \ \dfrac{3}{7}$ _____

30. $2\dfrac{1}{2}, \ \dfrac{7}{2}, \ 2\dfrac{1}{3}, \ 2\dfrac{4}{5}, \ 2\dfrac{3}{8}$ _____

Using the Strategies

Solve the problems below. You may want to make an organized list or draw pictures.

1. List all the ways to make $1 using at least one of each of the following coins: half dollar, quarter, dime, nickel, penny. How many different ways are there?

2. A car dealer received 5 new convertibles. Each car was a different color: red, white, black, green, and yellow. They will be displayed in the window 3 at a time. If the order is <u>not</u> considered, how many different ways can they be displayed? HINT: Black, white, red is the same as white, black, red.

3. There are 120 chairs divided between two rooms. In one room there are 36 more chairs than in the other room. How many chairs are there in each room?

4. Tricia has 3 T-shirts and 4 pairs of shorts. How many different outfits could she make from these choices?

5. Venessa, Chris, and Adam plan to sit together on the school bus, which holds 3 people per seat. How many different seating arrangements are possible? (Order <u>does</u> matter on this problem.) Use the chart below.

	Students' Names				
Window					
Center					
Aisle					

Adding and Subtracting Fractions

Add or subtract. Write the answer in lowest terms.

1. $\dfrac{5}{9} + \dfrac{3}{9}$ _____   **2.** $\dfrac{7}{12} - \dfrac{1}{12}$ _____   **3.** $\dfrac{9}{15} + \dfrac{1}{3}$ _____

4. $\dfrac{1}{5} + \dfrac{1}{6}$ _____   **5.** $\dfrac{3}{4} + \dfrac{5}{6}$ _____   **6.** $\dfrac{1}{8} + \dfrac{2}{3}$ _____

7. $\dfrac{3}{4} - \dfrac{5}{8}$ _____   **8.** $\dfrac{5}{6} - \dfrac{2}{3}$ _____   **9.** $\dfrac{5}{8} - \dfrac{1}{8}$ _____

10.
$$\begin{array}{r} \frac{5}{6} \\ -\ \frac{5}{9} \\ \hline \end{array}$$

11.
$$\begin{array}{r} \frac{5}{8} \\ +\ \frac{3}{4} \\ \hline \end{array}$$

12.
$$\begin{array}{r} \frac{3}{4} \\ -\ \frac{1}{2} \\ \hline \end{array}$$

13.
$$\begin{array}{r} \frac{2}{3} \\ +\ \frac{5}{6} \\ \hline \end{array}$$

14.
$$\begin{array}{r} \frac{5}{9} \\ -\ \frac{1}{2} \\ \hline \end{array}$$

15.
$$\begin{array}{r} \frac{2}{3} \\ +\ \frac{1}{10} \\ \hline \end{array}$$

16.
$$\begin{array}{r} \frac{5}{6} \\ -\ \frac{3}{8} \\ \hline \end{array}$$

17.
$$\begin{array}{r} \frac{1}{4} \\ +\ \frac{1}{3} \\ \hline \end{array}$$

18.
$$\begin{array}{r} \frac{8}{9} \\ -\ \frac{2}{3} \\ \hline \end{array}$$

Simplify the expression.

19. $\left(2\dfrac{5}{7} + \dfrac{3}{14}\right) - \dfrac{1}{2}$ _____   **20.** $\left(1\dfrac{2}{3} - \dfrac{1}{4}\right) + \dfrac{1}{6}$ _____

Name _____

Estimating Sums and Differences

Estimate each sum or difference. Use rounding.

1. $1\frac{1}{2} + 2\frac{3}{4}$ _____

2. $3\frac{1}{5} - \frac{2}{3}$ _____

3. $\frac{2}{3} + 2\frac{1}{3}$ _____

4. $3\frac{2}{5} - \frac{4}{7}$ _____

5. $1\frac{1}{5} + 3\frac{1}{4}$ _____

6. $9\frac{1}{2} - \frac{3}{4}$ _____

7. $1\frac{5}{6} + 2\frac{1}{5}$ _____

8. $7\frac{12}{21} - 6\frac{1}{4}$ _____

9. $5\frac{13}{24} + 23\frac{5}{8}$ _____

10. $12\frac{1}{3} - \frac{1}{5}$ _____

11. $41\frac{3}{24} + 8\frac{17}{19}$ _____

12. $1\frac{1}{5} - \frac{1}{4}$ _____

13. $16\frac{3}{11} + \frac{1}{3}$ _____

14. $19\frac{3}{5} + \frac{1}{3}$ _____

15. $5\frac{9}{10} + \frac{7}{8}$ _____

16. $6\frac{2}{8} - 4\frac{3}{7}$ _____

17. $1\frac{1}{3} + \frac{1}{6}$ _____

18. $99\frac{7}{9} - 1\frac{3}{7}$ _____

19. $5\frac{1}{4} + 2\frac{1}{3}$ _____

20. $6\frac{7}{15} - 1\frac{1}{2}$ _____

21. $4\frac{5}{7} + \frac{2}{15}$ _____

22. $1\frac{3}{5} + 2\frac{2}{3} + 7\frac{1}{4}$ _____

23. $21\frac{1}{5} - 12\frac{2}{3} - \frac{1}{4}$ _____

24. $6\frac{3}{4} + 2\frac{1}{5} + 7\frac{3}{7}$ _____

25. $100\frac{1}{7} - 42\frac{4}{5} - \frac{9}{10}$ _____

26. $13\frac{1}{3} + \frac{2}{3} + 3\frac{1}{3}$ _____

27. $47\frac{1}{2} - \frac{3}{4} - 2\frac{1}{3}$ _____

28. $(2\frac{1}{3} + 7\frac{1}{5}) - 3\frac{3}{4}$ _____

29. $(23\frac{3}{5} - 2\frac{1}{9}) + 6\frac{4}{7}$ _____

30. $(4\frac{1}{4} + 3\frac{1}{3}) - 1\frac{1}{2}$ _____

31. $(17\frac{2}{5} - 3\frac{1}{2}) + 4\frac{1}{3}$ _____

32. $(4\frac{4}{9} + 6\frac{6}{7}) - 2\frac{1}{3}$ _____

33. $(27\frac{1}{2} - 3\frac{3}{5}) + 6$ _____

Use with text pages 164–165.

Adding Mixed Numbers

Add. Write the answer in lowest terms.

1. $5\frac{4}{5}$
     $+\ 3\frac{1}{3}$
     _____

2. $7\frac{1}{2}$
     $+\ 6\frac{5}{6}$
     _____

3. $2\frac{3}{10}$
     $+\ 1\frac{3}{5}$
     _____

4. $2\frac{1}{6}$
     $+\ \frac{1}{3}$
     _____

5. $8\frac{3}{5}$
     $+\ 5\frac{7}{10}$
     _____

6. $5\frac{3}{8}$
     $+\ 4\frac{1}{3}$
     _____

7. $68\frac{3}{10}$
     $+\ 24\frac{1}{5}$
     _____

8. $72\frac{13}{16}$
     $+\ 8\frac{3}{4}$
     _____

9. $50\frac{3}{32}$
     $+\ 82\frac{1}{2}$
     _____

10. $1\frac{1}{2}$
      $2\frac{1}{4}$
      $+\ 3\frac{1}{8}$
      _____

11. $9\frac{1}{3}$
      $8\frac{1}{2}$
      $+\ 5\frac{5}{6}$
      _____

12. $16\frac{1}{4}$
      $12\frac{1}{16}$
      $+\ 9\frac{3}{8}$
      _____

13. $2\frac{2}{3}$
      $7\frac{1}{2}$
      $+\ 6\frac{5}{6}$
      _____

14. $42\frac{1}{2}$
      $7\frac{3}{8}$
      $+\ 11\frac{1}{16}$
      _____

15. $29\frac{2}{5}$
      $77\frac{3}{10}$
      $+\ 8\frac{1}{4}$
      _____

Subtracting Mixed Numbers

Subtract. Write the answer in lowest terms.

1. $9\frac{2}{3}$
$-\ 3\frac{4}{5}$
_____

2. 7
$-\ 5\frac{9}{10}$
_____

3. $6\frac{3}{8}$
$-\ 2\frac{7}{12}$
_____

4. $8\frac{1}{2}$
$-\ 1\frac{3}{4}$
_____

5. $4\frac{1}{5}$
$-\ 2\frac{7}{8}$
_____

6. 11
$-\ 9\frac{5}{7}$
_____

7. 40
$-\ 16\frac{2}{3}$
_____

8. $12\frac{1}{4}$
$-\ 3\frac{7}{10}$
_____

9. $52\frac{3}{4}$
$-\ 36\frac{5}{6}$
_____

10. $28\frac{83}{100}$
$-\ 15\frac{7}{10}$
_____

11. 66
$-\ 12\frac{5}{8}$
_____

12. $86\frac{7}{9}$
$-\ 31\frac{5}{6}$
_____

13. $32\frac{5}{6}$
$-\ 17\frac{3}{4}$
_____

14. $9\frac{1}{6}$
$-\ 4\frac{5}{8}$
_____

15. $46\frac{1}{3}$
$-\ 18\frac{1}{2}$
_____

Using the Strategies

Solve. Use Draw a Picture, Make a Table, or Look for a Pattern.

1. A skydiver jumps from a plane. After 1 minute he has fallen 20 feet, after 2 minutes he has fallen 50 feet, after 3 minutes he has fallen 90 feet, and so on. How many feet has he fallen after 6 minutes?

_____

2. The ski trip has to be canceled. All 28 people must be told. In the first hour 2 people each call 2 people. The next hour each of the people called the hour before calls 2 people, and so on. How many hours will it take for all 28 people to be called?

_____

3. Hillside Little League has 12 teams. Each team plays each of the other teams twice. How many games are played?

_____

4. The arts and crafts exhibit at the county fair costs $6 for 1 adult. Mr. Hill, his wife, and their 3 children paid $22.50 to get in. How much does each child's ticket cost?

_____

5. Rebecca cannot remember her friend's apartment number. She does remember it has the digits 3, 4, and 7. What apartment numbers are possible?

_____

6. Yukio and his 5 friends want to keep in touch during winter vacation. If they each speak to everyone in their group once during the week, how many calls will be made?

_____

7. Mrs. Manning has 3 daughters and 2 sons. Each of her daughters has 2 sons and a daughter and each of her sons has 3 daughters and a son. How many grandchildren does Mrs. Manning have?

_____

8. How many of Mrs. Manning's

grandchildren are girls? _____

How many are boys? _____

Discovering Methods of Computing

Use ICON's method to add or subtract fractions.
Write the numbers to show your thinking.

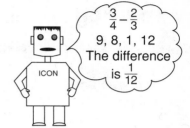

$\frac{3}{4} - \frac{2}{3}$
9, 8, 1, 12
The difference is $\frac{1}{12}$

1. $\frac{2}{3} + \frac{1}{4}$

_____

2. $\frac{3}{4} + \frac{1}{6}$

_____

3. $\frac{3}{10} + \frac{1}{6}$

_____

4. $\frac{3}{4} - \frac{1}{2}$

_____

5. $\frac{3}{4} - \frac{1}{6}$

_____

6. $\frac{4}{5} - \frac{1}{4}$

_____

7. $\frac{1}{3} + \frac{1}{2}$

_____

8. $\frac{1}{2} - \frac{1}{3}$

_____

9. $\frac{5}{8} + \frac{1}{6}$

_____

10. $\frac{3}{8} - \frac{1}{6}$

_____

11. $\frac{2}{3} + \frac{1}{6}$

_____

12. $\frac{5}{6} - \frac{1}{9}$

_____

13. $\frac{1}{3} + \frac{1}{4}$

_____

14. $\frac{2}{3} - \frac{1}{2}$

_____

15. $\frac{5}{7} + \frac{3}{8}$

_____

Name _____

Exploring Algebra: Thinking About Functions

Decide whether each relationship is a function. Explain your answer.

1.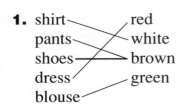

_____

_____

2.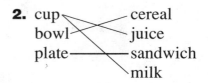

_____

_____

3.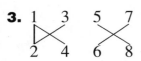

_____

_____

4. 1   3   5   7   9
| ╳   ╳
2   4   6   8

_____

_____

5.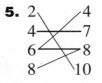

_____

_____

6.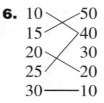

_____

_____

7.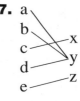

_____

_____

Tell whether the relationship that matches the first number to the second in the ordered pair is a function.

8. (1, 3) (2, 5) (3, 7) (4, 9)

9. (1, 1) (2, 1) (3, 2) (4, 2)

_____

10. (5, 1) (4, 2) (3, 3) (5, 4)

11. (4, 1) (4, 2) (4, 3) (4, 4)

_____

Multiplying Fractions and Whole Numbers

Find the given fraction of each number.

1. $\frac{1}{2} \times 16$ = _____

2. $\frac{2}{3} \times 24$ = _____

3. $\frac{4}{5}$ of 35 = _____

4. $\frac{1}{4} \times 36$ = _____

5. $\frac{2}{7} \times 49$ = _____

6. $\frac{1}{6} \times 42$ = _____

7. $\frac{4}{9}$ of 90 = _____

8. $\frac{5}{8} \times 80$ = _____

9. $\frac{1}{10} \times 10$ = _____

10. $\frac{5}{12} \times 36$ = _____

11. $\frac{3}{4}$ of 48 = _____

12. $\frac{3}{16} \times 48$ = _____

13. $\frac{3}{7} \times 56$ = _____

14. $\frac{1}{8}$ of 24 = _____

15. $\frac{2}{5} \times 50$ = _____

16. $\frac{1}{3} \times 72$ = _____

17. $\frac{3}{10} \times 40$ = _____

18. $\frac{5}{9} \times 63$ = _____

19. $\frac{1}{100} \times 600$ = _____

20. $\frac{1}{5} \times 100$ = _____

21. $\frac{4}{7} \times 70$ = _____

22. $\frac{5}{6} \times 54$ = _____

23. $\frac{5}{16} \times 32$ = _____

24. $\frac{3}{8} \times 56$ = _____

25. $\frac{2}{9}$ of 54 = _____

26. $\frac{1}{7} \times 35$ = _____

27. $\frac{9}{10} \times 80$ = _____

28. $\frac{3}{5} \times 20$ = _____

29. $\frac{2}{25}$ of 50 = _____

30. $\frac{6}{7} \times 77$ = _____

Name _____

Multiplying Fractions

Multiply. Use the shortcut whenever possible.

1. $\frac{1}{2} \times \frac{1}{7} =$ _____

2. $\frac{1}{8} \times \frac{1}{3} =$ _____

3. $\frac{1}{5} \times \frac{1}{8} =$ _____

4. $\frac{1}{3} \times \frac{1}{3} =$ _____

5. $\frac{1}{4} \times \frac{1}{10} =$ _____

6. $\frac{1}{2} \times \frac{1}{100} =$ _____

7. $\frac{1}{2} \times \frac{3}{5} =$ _____

8. $\frac{7}{10} \times \frac{5}{6} =$ _____

9. $\frac{1}{10} \times \frac{3}{10} =$ _____

10. $\frac{3}{4} \times \frac{1}{3} =$ _____

11. $\frac{2}{3} \times \frac{9}{10} =$ _____

12. $\frac{4}{5} \times \frac{7}{12} =$ _____

13. $\frac{2}{5} \times \frac{2}{5} =$ _____

14. $\frac{5}{9} \times \frac{3}{2} =$ _____

15. $\frac{49}{100} \times \frac{4}{7} =$ _____

16. $\frac{2}{5} \times \frac{1}{2} =$ _____

17. $\frac{5}{6} \times \frac{3}{10} =$ _____

18. $\frac{5}{6} \times \frac{6}{5} =$ _____

19. $\frac{9}{10} \times \frac{1}{3} =$ _____

20. $\frac{2}{3} \times \frac{3}{4} =$ _____

21. $\frac{9}{10} \times \frac{2}{3} =$ _____

22. $\frac{7}{8} \times \frac{4}{5} =$ _____

23. $\frac{3}{8} \times \frac{2}{3} =$ _____

24. $\frac{1}{2} \times \frac{7}{8} =$ _____

25. $\frac{3}{4} \times \frac{4}{3} \times \frac{2}{3} =$ _____

26. $\frac{3}{4} \times \frac{3}{8} \times \frac{2}{3} =$ _____

27. $\frac{5}{6} \times 3 \times \frac{1}{2} =$ _____

28. $\frac{1}{3} \times \frac{3}{4} \times \frac{2}{3} =$ _____

29. $\frac{3}{4} \times \frac{1}{2} \times \frac{1}{5} =$ _____

30. $\frac{8}{6} \times \frac{3}{4} \times 4 =$ _____

Multiplying Mixed Numbers

Multiply. Express the product in lowest terms.

1. $2\frac{2}{3} \times \frac{3}{5}$ = _____

2. $1\frac{1}{4} \times 6\frac{2}{3}$ = _____

3. $2\frac{3}{4} \times 4$ = _____

4. $1\frac{1}{4} \times 3$ = _____

5. $2\frac{1}{2} \times \frac{1}{5}$ = _____

6. $\frac{2}{3} \times 2\frac{1}{2}$ = _____

7. $\frac{1}{3} \times 3\frac{3}{4}$ = _____

8. $2\frac{4}{7} \times 3\frac{2}{3}$ = _____

9. $6\frac{3}{4} \times 3$ = _____

10. $5 \times 3\frac{1}{2}$ = _____

11. $9\frac{6}{7} \times \frac{1}{10}$ = _____

12. $10\frac{5}{12} \times 3\frac{1}{5}$ = _____

13. $2\frac{1}{2} \times 2\frac{1}{2}$ = _____

14. $1\frac{2}{3} \times 2\frac{3}{5} \times 1\frac{1}{8}$ = _____

15. $3\frac{1}{2} \times 1\frac{1}{4} \times \frac{4}{5}$ = _____

16. $4\frac{2}{3} \times 2\frac{1}{3} \times 1\frac{1}{2}$ = _____

17. $2\frac{4}{5} \times 6\frac{1}{2} \times \frac{5}{7}$ = _____

18. $3\frac{3}{4} \times \frac{4}{15} \times \frac{2}{3}$ = _____

Estimate each product.

19. $4\frac{1}{6} \times 3\frac{1}{4}$ = _____

20. $\frac{5}{6} \times 3\frac{3}{4}$ = _____

21. $10\frac{1}{8} \times 4\frac{4}{5}$ = _____

22. $8\frac{3}{4} \times 4\frac{1}{3} \times 2\frac{1}{3}$ = _____

23. $3\frac{4}{5} \times 2\frac{1}{3} \times 2\frac{2}{3}$ = _____

24. $7\frac{1}{4} \times 3\frac{3}{8} \times \frac{2}{3}$ = _____

Name _____

Dividing Fractions

Divide. Express your answer in lowest terms.

1. $\dfrac{1}{4} \div \dfrac{3}{4}$ = _____

2. $\dfrac{2}{3} \div \dfrac{2}{5}$ = _____

3. $\dfrac{1}{2} \div \dfrac{3}{4}$ = _____

4. $\dfrac{1}{6} \div \dfrac{1}{2}$ = _____

5. $\dfrac{4}{5} \div \dfrac{2}{5}$ = _____

6. $\dfrac{3}{4} \div \dfrac{5}{6}$ = _____

7. $\dfrac{7}{8} \div \dfrac{1}{4}$ = _____

8. $\dfrac{8}{21} \div \dfrac{2}{7}$ = _____

9. $\dfrac{4}{27} \div \dfrac{4}{9}$ = _____

10. $\dfrac{5}{6} \div \dfrac{1}{3}$ = _____

11. $\dfrac{24}{100} \div \dfrac{1}{4}$ = _____

12. $\dfrac{18}{25} \div \dfrac{3}{5}$ = _____

13. $\dfrac{7}{10} \div \dfrac{1}{2}$ = _____

14. $\dfrac{5}{3} \div \dfrac{1}{3}$ = _____

15. $\dfrac{9}{16} \div \dfrac{3}{8}$ = _____

16. $\dfrac{5}{12} \div \dfrac{1}{6}$ = _____

17. $\dfrac{1}{3} \div \dfrac{5}{6}$ = _____

18. $\dfrac{5}{8} \div \dfrac{5}{16}$ = _____

19. $\dfrac{5}{6} \div \dfrac{2}{3}$ = _____

20. $\dfrac{1}{12} \div \dfrac{3}{8}$ = _____

21. $\dfrac{4}{14} \div \dfrac{4}{7}$ = _____

22. $\dfrac{7}{12} \div \dfrac{1}{15}$ = _____

23. $\dfrac{5}{9} \div \dfrac{1}{2}$ = _____

24. $\dfrac{9}{10} \div \dfrac{2}{5}$ = _____

25. Find the quotient when $\dfrac{9}{12}$ is divided by $\dfrac{3}{4}$. _____

Use with text pages 182–183.

Dividing Mixed Numbers

Divide. Express your answer in lowest terms.

1. $5\frac{1}{5} \div 1\frac{3}{10} =$ _____

2. $8 \div 2\frac{1}{2} =$ _____

3. $6\frac{2}{3} \div 2\frac{1}{6} =$ _____

4. $12 \div 1\frac{1}{2} =$ _____

5. $5\frac{1}{3} \div 2\frac{2}{3} =$ _____

6. $1\frac{7}{8} \div 2\frac{1}{4} =$ _____

7. $3\frac{1}{2} \div \frac{1}{10} =$ _____

8. $2\frac{3}{4} \div 1\frac{3}{8} =$ _____

9. $\frac{5}{6} \div 2\frac{1}{3} =$ _____

10. $1\frac{3}{4} \div \frac{7}{8} =$ _____

11. $\frac{9}{10} \div 5\frac{2}{5} =$ _____

12. $2\frac{5}{8} \div \frac{7}{12} =$ _____

13. $9\frac{1}{3} \div \frac{14}{15} =$ _____

14. $14 \div 3\frac{1}{2} =$ _____

15. $1\frac{2}{3} \div \frac{5}{6} =$ _____

16. $1\frac{1}{2} \div 2\frac{3}{5} =$ _____

17. $3\frac{1}{2} \div 1\frac{1}{2} =$ _____

18. $3\frac{1}{2} \div 1\frac{2}{5} =$ _____

Estimate each quotient.

19. $2\frac{3}{4} \div 2\frac{1}{2} =$ _____

20. $13\frac{7}{8} \div 2\frac{1}{3} =$ _____

21. $6\frac{3}{4} \div 3 =$ _____

22. $11\frac{2}{3} \div 3\frac{2}{3} =$ _____

23. $5\frac{1}{2} \div \frac{1}{2} =$ _____

24. $32\frac{4}{5} \div 9\frac{1}{2} =$ _____

Name _____

Determining Reasonable Answers

Number of Students at Hamilton Valley School	
Grade 6	420 students
Grade 7	393 students
Grade 8	245 students

Do not solve the first two problems. Decide if the answer given is reasonable. If it is not reasonable, explain why.

1. The cafeteria orders 5 containers of milk for each student every week. How many containers must be ordered for the week?
500 containers

_____

_____

_____

2. The school is buying new bleachers for the field. Each bleacher section holds 200 students. How many sections are needed for all students?
6 sections

_____

_____

_____

Solve.

3. The seventh grade is planning a bus trip. Each bus holds 48 students. How many buses will be needed?

_____

4. Each day half the school's students walk to school. The other half ride school buses. How many students walk to school?

_____

5. The seventh and eighth grade picnic is held every spring. Each student may buy two tickets. If all seventh and eighth graders buy them, how many tickets will be sold?

_____

6. Of the total number of students, 548 are girls. How many boys attend the school?

_____

7. Each seventh grade math class may have no more than 26 students. How many math classes are needed for all seventh graders?

_____

Algebraic Expressions: Addition and Subraction

Write word phrases for these algebraic
expressions or diagrams.

1. $17 - n$ _____

2.  _____

3.  _____

4. $\$14.23 + \$1.49 + n$ _____

5. $n - 45$ _____

6. 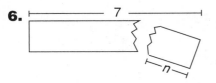 _____

Write algebraic expressions for these word phrases.

7. 9 minus a number d _____

8. 7 more than a number f _____

9. the sum of a number p
and 9 _____

10. 75 decreased by a
number l _____

11. 2 less than a number j _____

12. 8 more than a number k _____

13. a number e more than 6 _____

14. 12 minus a number w _____

15. a number t minus 30 _____

16. 18 more than a number c _____

17. 39 added to a number u _____

18. a number a minus 15 _____

19. 42 plus a number g _____

20. a number v plus 8 _____

21. a number r minus 10 _____

22. 57 minus a number q _____

Algebraic Expressions: Multiplication and Division

Write an algebraic expression and draw a diagram for
each situation.

1. length *l* divided by 4

_____

2. length *l* divided by 6

_____

3. eight times as much money as *d* dollars

_____

4. a jump 5 times as high as *j*

_____

Write an algebraic expression that tells you how many:

5. feet are in *m* miles

_____

6. seconds are in *m* minutes

_____

7. dimes are in *d* dollars

_____

8. inches are in *f* feet

_____

Write an algebraic expression that tells you how to change:

9. *w* weeks into years

_____

10. *o* ounces into pounds

_____

11. *g* grams into kilograms

_____

12. *c* centimeters into meters

_____

Translating Phrases into Algebraic Expressions

Translate each situation into an algebraic expression.

1. Lana went to the matinee performance at the local theater. The theater was full. Let n be the number of people at the theater. Write an expression that tells how many people would have been at the matinee if $\frac{1}{2}$ as many were there.

_____

2. Lana bought a glass of pineapple juice during intermission. Her friend bought twice as much juice. Let j be the amount of juice Lana bought. Write an expression that tells how much juice her friend bought.

_____

3. Theater tickets now cost 8 times as much as they did when Lana's grandmother was a child. Write an expression that tells how much Lana paid for her ticket. Let t be the amount Lana's grandmother paid.

_____

4. At the matinee performance, 13 people had to stand because all the seats were taken. Let s be the number of people with seats. Write an expression that tells how many people in all were at the performance.

_____

5. 27 more than a number y

_____

6. The product of a number p and 12

_____

Solving Equations Using Objects

Use objects to find what ⊠ stands for in terms of chips.
Remember: ○ stands for "subtract 1"
                     ● stands for "add 1"
                     ⊠ stands for "unknown value"

1. ⊠ ○ | ● ●
                ● ●

_____
_____

2. ⊠ ● | ●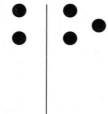

_____
_____

3. ⊠ | ● ●
         ○ ○ | ● ● ●
                    ●

_____
_____

4. ⊠ ⊠ | ○ ○
         ⊠ ● | ○ ○
                    ○ ○ ○

_____
_____

5. ⊠ | ● ●
         ⊠ ● | ● ●
                 ● | ● ●

_____
_____

6. ⊠ ⊠ | ○ ○
                    ○ ○

_____
_____

6. ⊠ ● | ○ ○
         ● ● | ○ ○
         ⊠ ●

_____
_____

7. ⊠ | ⊠
         ○ | ●
         ⊠

_____
_____

8. ⊠ | ⊠ ⊠
         ○ ⊠ | ○ ○
         ○ ⊠ | ○

_____
_____

Analyzing Data to Discover a Pattern

Look for a pattern. Complete each table.

1.

Miles	Cost
10	$20
12	$22
18	$28
24	
34	

2.

Hours	Number of Pages
4	12
6	18
	21
9	
	36

3.

Hours	Number Inspected
2	4
12	
42	84
134	
408	

4.

Pounds	Cost
1	$12
2	
3	$14
4	
5	

5.

Days	Number Bought
3	2
9	8
27	
	80
243	

6.

km	Cost
9	$16
12	$19
17	
21	
	$32

7.

Factories	Number Installed
2	100
5	250
8	
11	550
	700

8.

Minutes	Number Stamped
1	100
3	300
12	
60	6,000
	3,600

9.

Days	Number Delivered
8	20
12	
16	36
20	44
24	

Solving Equations and Mental Math

Use mental math to solve each equation.

1. $x + 69 = 69$, $x =$ _____

2. $y - 60 = 30$, $y =$ _____

3. $12y = 60$, $y =$ _____

4. $\frac{s}{4} = 7$, $s =$ _____

5. $85 + b = 100$, $b =$ _____

6. $5z = 125$, $z =$ _____

7. $\frac{p}{100} = 1$, $p =$ _____

8. $c + 5 = 42$, $c =$ _____

9. $r - 46 = 56$, $r =$ _____

10. $118 + t = 123.4$, $t =$ _____

11. $42y = 0$, $y =$ _____

12. $66 - q = 22$, $q =$ _____

13. $\frac{n}{3} = 0.667$, $n =$ _____

14. $f - 44 = 55$, $f =$ _____

15. $d + 76 = 90$, $d =$ _____

16. $\frac{18}{n} = 18$, $n =$ _____

Decide which equations can be solved using mental math. Solve only those equations.

17. $12z = 120$

_____

18. $\frac{a}{15} = 3$

_____

19. $\frac{2}{5}y = 34.4$

_____

20. $m + 19 = 20.8$

_____

21. $\frac{1}{8}z = 12$

_____

22. $423 - y = 399$

_____

23. $1.4k = 2.24$

_____

24. $53 - d = 25$

_____

Problem Solving: Using Guess and Check to Solve Equations

Solve. Use Guess and Check.

1. $r + 56 = 103$

$r =$ _____

2. $\frac{s}{5} = 13$

$s =$ _____

3. $9t = 126$

$t =$ _____

4. $78 - u = 19$

$u =$ _____

5. $47 + v = 256$

$v =$ _____

6. $\frac{168}{w} = 12$

$w =$ _____

Solve the equation with Guess and Check. Use a complete sentence to answer the question.

7. On her way home from work, Mrs. Santos picked up $22.50 worth of movie tickets for her son and his 4 friends. How much do each of the teenagers owe her?

Let c be the cost of each ticket.
Solve $5c = 22.50$ to find the cost of 1 ticket.

$c =$ _____ _____

8. Claes paid $15 for a model plane kit. He sold the finished plane and made a profit of $6. What did he charge for the finished plane?

Let m be the price of the finished plane.
Solve $m - 15 = 6$ to find the price of the finished plane.

$m =$ _____ _____

9. Vilma added 17 new shells to her collection. That brought the total number of shells she had to 84. How many shells did she have originally?

Let s be the original number of shells.
Solve $s + 17 = 84$ to find the original number of shells.

$s =$ _____ _____

Inverse Operations

Write an algebraic expression for each picture.
Then give the inverse operation that would get the
variable alone.

1.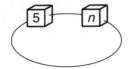

_____

2.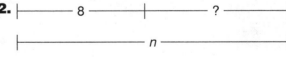

_____

3.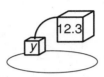

_____

4.

_____

Write an algebraic expression for each phrase. Then
give the inverse operation that would get the variable alone.

5. l less 75

_____

6. c plus 84

_____

7. 5 more than z

_____

Simplify each expression. Then give the inverse
operation that would get the variable alone.

8. $(x + 3) - 5$

_____

9. $(x - 3) + 5$

_____

10. $(5 - 3) + x$

_____

11. $(y + 3.26) - 2.26$

_____

12. $(2.055 + a) + 0.055$

_____

13. $(b - 8.9) + 17.8$

_____

Name _____

Solving Addition and Subtraction Equations

Solve and check.

1. $a - 48 = 563$

_____

2. $z + 18.9 = 26.3$

_____

3. $v - 4 = 8.76$

_____

4. $b - 2\frac{3}{4} = 1\frac{1}{4}$

_____

5. $m + 76 = 333$

_____

6. $7 + y = 7$

_____

7. $x + 23\frac{1}{3} = 354$

_____

8. $354 + x = 423\frac{1}{3}$

_____

9. $b + 18 = 46.9$

_____

10. $t + 18.7 = 53$

_____

11. $65.13 + r = 89.7$

_____

12. $z + 0 = 0$

_____

13. $v - 8.2 = 16.4$

_____

14. $424 = s + 86$

_____

15. $n - 5 = 5$

_____

16. $49\frac{3}{2} + t = 300$

_____

17. $5.555 + n = 15$

_____

18. $x + 0.4 = 5.1$

_____

More Inverse Operations

Give the inverse operation that would get the
variable alone.

1. $\frac{x}{54}$

_____

2. $27.43y$

_____

3. $m \div 47$

_____

4. $13.42n$

_____

5. $\overline{0\ 2}$.

_____

6. $434a$

_____

7. $\frac{z}{14}$

_____

8. $74.5b$

_____

9. $\frac{d}{123}$

_____

Write an algebraic expression for each. Then give
the inverse operation that would get the variable
alone.

10. 4.6 times longer than l

_____

11. diameter d divided by 12.2

_____

12. 7 times q quarters

_____

13. $\frac{1}{3}$ the age of Vinnie (v)

_____

14. $\frac{1}{2}$ as far as m miles

_____

15. 76 times the width w

_____

Name _____

Solving Multiplication and Division Equations

Solve and check.

1. $4h = 112$

_____

2. $v \div 47 = 96$

_____

3. $43n = 301$

_____

4. $18f = 504$

_____

5. $\frac{t}{21} = 21$

_____

6. $\frac{a}{63} = 5{,}607$

_____

7. $30b = 1{,}308$

_____

8. $\frac{m}{48} = 11.2$

_____

9. $\frac{918}{j} = 18$

_____

10. $\frac{w}{9} = 477$

_____

11. $5.5k = 0$

_____

12. $4.324z = 4.324$

_____

13. $103m = 10{,}609$

_____

14. $\frac{1{,}000}{n} = 250$

_____

15. $\frac{h}{28} = 34$

_____

16. $8c = 4{,}896$

_____

17. $\frac{l}{12} = 12$

_____

18. $0.125z = 80$

_____

Ratio

Write each ratio as a fraction in lowest terms.

1. 2 to 4 _____

2. 15:25 _____

3. $\frac{45}{36}$ _____

4. $\frac{18}{32}$ _____

5. 14 to 18 _____

6. 14:12 _____

7. 18:9 _____

8. $\frac{14}{21}$ _____

9. 30 to 24 _____

10. 16 to 14 _____

11. 24:16 _____

12. $\frac{8}{6}$ _____

13. $\frac{8}{12}$ _____

14. 27 to 36 _____

15. 4:16 _____

16. 9:12 _____

17. $\frac{25}{15}$ _____

18. 15 to 27 _____

19. 81 to 45 _____

20. 16:12 _____

21. $\frac{40}{16}$ _____

22. $\frac{21}{18}$ _____

23. 8 to 14 _____

24. 18:48 _____

25. 30 to 36 _____

26. $\frac{30}{25}$ _____

27. 63:14 _____

28. $\frac{32}{36}$ _____

29. 42 to 12 _____

30. 24:64 _____

31. 81 to 27 _____

32. $\frac{9}{6}$ _____

33. 12 to 8 _____

Proportions

Write = or ≠ for each $\bigcirc$. Use cross products to decide.

1. $\dfrac{8}{24}$ $\bigcirc$ $\dfrac{4}{10}$ **2.** $\dfrac{5}{8}$ $\bigcirc$ $\dfrac{6}{9}$ **3.** $\dfrac{6}{14}$ $\bigcirc$ $\dfrac{3}{7}$

4. $\dfrac{2}{3}$ $\bigcirc$ $\dfrac{8}{12}$ **5.** $\dfrac{3}{5}$ $\bigcirc$ $\dfrac{7}{10}$ **6.** $\dfrac{1}{2}$ $\bigcirc$ $\dfrac{5}{11}$

7. $\dfrac{9}{10}$ $\bigcirc$ $\dfrac{18}{20}$ **8.** $\dfrac{9}{15}$ $\bigcirc$ $\dfrac{3}{5}$ **9.** $\dfrac{12}{16}$ $\bigcirc$ $\dfrac{3}{4}$

10. $\dfrac{5}{7}$ $\bigcirc$ $\dfrac{6}{8}$ **11.** $\dfrac{5}{11}$ $\bigcirc$ $\dfrac{2}{20}$ **12.** $\dfrac{4}{9}$ $\bigcirc$ $\dfrac{8}{18}$

13. $\dfrac{20}{16}$ $\bigcirc$ $\dfrac{15}{12}$ **14.** $\dfrac{8}{10}$ $\bigcirc$ $\dfrac{4}{5}$ **15.** $\dfrac{21}{4}$ $\bigcirc$ $\dfrac{13}{3}$

16. $\dfrac{7}{5}$ $\bigcirc$ $\dfrac{5}{2}$ **17.** $\dfrac{24}{6}$ $\bigcirc$ $\dfrac{8}{2}$ **18.** $\dfrac{9}{5}$ $\bigcirc$ $\dfrac{27}{15}$

19. $\dfrac{3}{5}$ $\bigcirc$ $\dfrac{6}{10}$ **20.** $\dfrac{4}{6}$ $\bigcirc$ $\dfrac{6}{9}$ **21.** $\dfrac{3}{5}$ $\bigcirc$ $\dfrac{5}{4}$

22. $\dfrac{3}{4}$ $\bigcirc$ $\dfrac{7}{9}$ **23.** $\dfrac{7}{2}$ $\bigcirc$ $\dfrac{11}{3}$ **24.** $\dfrac{8}{48}$ $\bigcirc$ $\dfrac{3}{18}$

25. $\dfrac{7}{5}$ $\bigcirc$ $\dfrac{8}{6}$ **26.** $\dfrac{6}{12}$ $\bigcirc$ $\dfrac{9}{18}$ **27.** $\dfrac{5}{6}$ $\bigcirc$ $\dfrac{45}{54}$

28. $\dfrac{3}{8}$ $\bigcirc$ $\dfrac{32}{12}$ **29.** $\dfrac{3}{4}$ $\bigcirc$ $\dfrac{15}{20}$ **30.** $\dfrac{5}{7}$ $\bigcirc$ $\dfrac{35}{49}$

31. $\dfrac{4}{5}$ $\bigcirc$ $\dfrac{5}{4}$ **32.** $\dfrac{3}{7}$ $\bigcirc$ $\dfrac{5}{10}$ **33.** $\dfrac{2}{9}$ $\bigcirc$ $\dfrac{12}{54}$

Name _____

Solving Proportions

Solve the following proportions for n.

1. $\dfrac{2}{3} = \dfrac{6}{n}$ $n =$ _____

2. $\dfrac{4}{5} = \dfrac{n}{45}$ $n =$ _____

3. $\dfrac{n}{5} = \dfrac{6}{3}$ $n =$ _____

4. $\dfrac{12}{n} = \dfrac{11}{55}$ $n =$ _____

5. $\dfrac{13}{5} = \dfrac{39}{n}$ $n =$ _____

6. $\dfrac{7}{20} = \dfrac{35}{n}$ $n =$ _____

7. $\dfrac{5}{n} = \dfrac{8}{48}$ $n =$ _____

8. $\dfrac{23}{33} = \dfrac{n}{132}$ $n =$ _____

Write and solve a proportion for each problem.

9. Jeanette can walk 1 km in 11 minutes. How far can she walk in 55 minutes? Let $w =$ the distance she can walk in 55 minutes.

_____

10. On Mickey's block the ratio of trees to houses is 19:5. There are 15 houses. How many trees are there? Let $t =$ the number of trees.

_____

11. Carlos can ride his bike 30 km in 2 h. How far can he ride in 7 h? Let $n =$ the distance he can ride in 7 h.

_____

12. At Sarah's school the ratio of students to teachers is 94:3. If there are 752 students in the school, how many teachers are there? Let $t =$ the number of teachers.

_____

13. At Alice's school the ratio of library books to students is 11:1. If there are 13,838 books in the library, how many students are there? Let $s =$ the number of students.

_____

14. On George's block the ratio of cars to houses is 8:5. There are 32 cars. How many houses are there? Let $h =$ the number of houses.

_____

Rate

Find the unit rate.

1. $\dfrac{30 \text{ min}}{3 \text{ mi}}$ _____

2. $\dfrac{105 \text{ days}}{15 \text{ weeks}}$ _____

3. $\dfrac{\$666}{36 \text{ hr}}$ _____

4. $\dfrac{5{,}592 \text{ mi}}{233 \text{ gal}}$ _____

5. $\dfrac{520 \text{ mi}}{8 \text{ hr}}$ _____

6. $\dfrac{72 \text{ radios}}{36 \text{ homes}}$ _____

7. $\dfrac{\$65{,}000}{5 \text{ yr}}$ _____

8. $\dfrac{\$65}{10 \text{ tickets}}$ _____

9. $\dfrac{\$1}{4 \text{ oranges}}$ _____

10. $\dfrac{30 \text{ min}}{5 \text{ km}}$ _____

11. $\dfrac{486 \text{ km}}{18 \text{ hr}}$ _____

12. $\dfrac{\$189}{\text{dozen}}$ _____

Solve.

13. Ming worked 40 hours and earned $680 before taxes. How much does Ming earn an hour?

_____

14. Mrs. Mosse's history class is going to the museum. They paid $135 for 27 tickets. What was the cost of one ticket?

_____

15. A bricklayer can lay 384 bricks in 8 hours. How many bricks can he lay in an hour?

_____

16. Nina drives 120 miles in 3 hours. How many miles does she drive in a half hour?

_____

17. Limes are 4 for $1. How much does one lime cost?

_____

18. Mr. Doughgan bakes 720 muffins in 8 hours. How many muffins does he bake in one hour?

_____

Unit Pricing

Solve. Use proportions when appropriate.

1. A 2-week pass to the town swimming pool costs $35 and a daily pass costs $4. If Martha plans to go to the pool 8 times in 2 weeks, what type of pass should she purchase?

_____

2. At the grocery store, Mrs. Lloyd sees that 64 oz of orange juice cost $3.20 and 16 oz of orange juice cost $1.44. Which is the better buy?

_____

3. A dozen bran muffins cost $6 at Stew's Bakery. If you purchase them one at a time, they cost $0.80 each. Craig needs 8 muffins. Which would cost less, buying 8 or a dozen muffins?

_____

4. Sasha wants to buy a flower for her mother. A dozen carnations cost $4.80 and 4 roses cost $2. Which flower is the better buy if Sasha buys one flower?

_____

5. Hugh drove 228 miles and used 12 gallons of gas. Nicole drove 273 miles and used 13 gallons of gas. Whose car got better gas mileage per gallon?

_____

6. Rita's Grocery Store sells 12 cans of juice for $3. Marie's Grocery Store sells 20 cans of juice for $4.60. Which store offers the better buy?

_____

7. Tricia worked 14 hours and earned $46.90. Jeff worked 12 hours and earned $40.80. Who earned more money per hour?

_____

8. Clayton paid $3.60 to have a roll of 24-exposure film developed. Gwen paid $4.32 to have a roll of 36-exposure film developed. Who paid less per picture?

_____

9. A monthly train pass costs $99. A daily one-way ticket costs $4.50. If Nancy makes 12 round-trip rides on the train in one month, should she purchase a monthly pass or daily passes?

_____

10. Oak Street has 12 homes and 60 residents living there. Maple Street has 8 homes and 32 residents living there. Which street has more residents per home?

_____

Name _____

Using Critical Thinking: Making Judgments

Use a calculator to find the ratio of the larger side (length)
to the smaller side (width) of the rectangle. Round answers
to the nearest thousandth.

1.   2
      3
_____

2.   4
      6
_____

3.   5
      8
_____

4.   7
      9
_____

5.   6
      10
_____

6.   6
      2
_____

7.   1
      2
_____

8.   5
      5
_____

9.   5
      3
_____

10.   8
      13
_____

11. Are any of your ratios close to the
    ratio of the Golden Rectangle–
    1.618:1? Which ones?

    _____

    _____

    _____

Scale Drawings

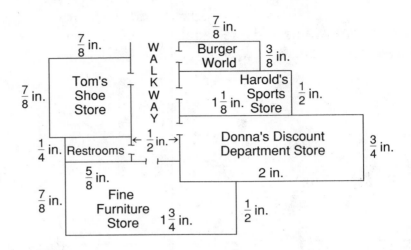

CROSSTOWN SHOPPING MALL

Scale: $\frac{1}{8}$ in. = 6 yd

Albert made a scale drawing of the mall. Use it to find the actual lengths and widths.

1. Tom's Shoe Store

$l =$ _____ $w =$ _____

2. Harold's Sports Store

$l =$ _____ $w =$ _____

3. Donna's Discount Store

$l =$ _____ $w =$ _____

4. Burger World

$l =$ _____ $w =$ _____

5. How many yards longer is Donna's Discount Store than Harold's Sports Store?

_____

6. How many yards wide is the walkway in the Crosstown Shopping Mall?

_____

7. What are the dimensions of the smallest area in the mall?

_____

8. What is the actual length of the wall between Harold's Sports Store and Burger World?

_____

Name _____

Exploring Algebra: Using Variables

Write the rule in words and as an algebraic expression.

1.

input	1	2	3	4	5	x
output	6	12	18	24	30	?

_____

_____

2.

input	1	2	3	4	5	q
output	1	3	5	7	9	?

_____

_____

3.

input	1	2	3	4	5	y
output	4	6	8	10	12	?

_____

_____

4.

hours worked	1	2	3	4	5	h
amount earned	7	12	17	22	27	?

_____

_____

5.

input	1	2	3	4	5	w
output	6	7	8	9	10	?

_____

_____

6.

input	1	2	3	4	5	n
output	$\frac{1}{2}$	1	$1\frac{1}{2}$	2	$2\frac{1}{2}$	?

_____

_____

7.

input	1	2	3	4	5	s
output	1	8	15	22	29	?

_____

_____

8.

miles	1	2	3	4	5	m
fare	1.25	2.50	3.75	5.00	6.25	?

_____

_____

Similar Figures

Find the length of x for each pair of similar figures.

1.

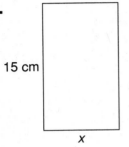

15 cm

10 cm

x

4 cm

$x = $ _____

2.

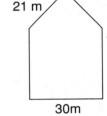

4 cm

12 cm

x

16 cm

$x = $ _____

3.

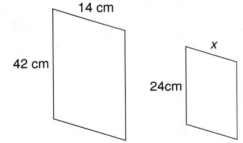

7m

3 cm

7m

x

$x = $ _____

4.

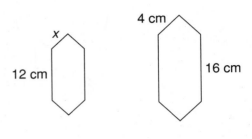

21 m

x

20m

30m

$x = $ _____

5.

14 cm

42 cm

x

24cm

$x = $ _____

6.

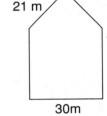

25 m

40 m

10 m

x

$x = $ _____

7.

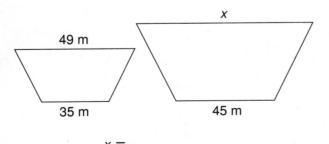

49 m

x

35 m

45 m

$x = $ _____

8.

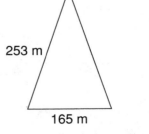

253 m

x

165 m

105 m

$x = $ _____

The Special Ratio π

Find the circumference, given each diameter or radius.
Use 3.14 or $\frac{22}{7}$ for π. You may use a calculator.

1. $d = 2$ cm _____

2. $r = 0.25$ m _____

3. $d = 51$ mm _____

4. $r = 14$ in. _____

5. $r = 6$ ft _____

6. $d = \frac{7}{8}$ yd _____

7. $d = 56$ mm _____

8. $d = 1.2$ m _____

9. $r = 17$ ft _____

10. $r = 7$ cm _____

Measure each diameter to the nearest mm.
Use 3.14 for π. Find the circumference of each circle
using $C = \pi d$.

	Diameter	Circumference
11.		
12.		
13.		
14.		

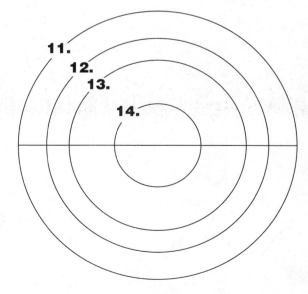

11.
12.
13.
14.

Using The Strategies

Solve. Use Guess and Check or Work Backward.

1. Four friends compared how much money they had for the summer camping trip. Carol had $54 more than Gina. John had $\frac{1}{3}$ as much as Gina. Denis had $11 more than Carol. John had $45. How much money did Denis have?

_____

2. Four students compared how many movies they saw over the summer. Bill saw 3 times as many as Brett. Amy saw 13 more than Brett. Sohara saw 1 more than Bill. Amy saw 15 movies. How many did Sohara see?

_____

3. Jim, Lynn, and Meish all ran in a 5-km race. Lynn took 3 minutes, 9 seconds longer than Jim. Jim ran 7 minutes, 40 seconds faster than Meish. Lynn finished the race in 29 minutes, 14 seconds. What was Meish's finishing time in the race?

_____

4. Tonya and Jordan are planning to hike to Great Rock. The hike is 12 miles. Tonya can hike 4 mph and Jordan can hike 6 mph. If they want to get to Great Rock at the same time, how much of a head start should Tonya have over Jordan?

_____

5. Marlene received shampoo samples as a promotion for a new product. She gave half of the samples to her family and 1 to a friend. She then gave half plus 1 of the remaining samples to her neighbors. She kept 4 for herself. How many samples did she receive?

_____

6. Anthony, Helene, Gene, and Richie organized a debate club at school. Helene brought in 4 less than half of the members. Richie brought in half as many as Helene. Gene brought in 4 more members than Richie. Richie brought in twice as many as Anthony. Anthony brought in 4 members. How many members besides the original 4 does the club have?

_____

7. New football equipment costs $620. Students contributed $\frac{1}{4}$; the PTA contributed $\frac{1}{5}$ of what was remaining after the students. A fund-raiser contributed $250 more than the PTA, and the principal paid $64 less than the PTA. How much did each contribute?

_____

_____

8. On a class trip 6 students visited the Gardens. Twice as many visited Water World. Of the remaining students, $\frac{1}{3}$ visited Fort Henry. Twice as many students visited the museum as the fort. 30 students went on the class trip. How many went to each attraction?

_____

_____

Percent

What percent of each square is shaded?

1.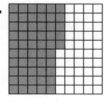

_____

2.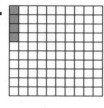

_____

3.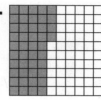

_____

4.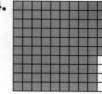

_____

5.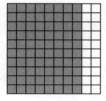

_____

6.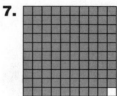

_____

7.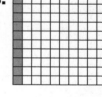

_____

8.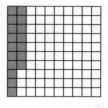

_____

	Ratio	Fraction	Decimal	Percent
9.	5 to 100			
10.	90 to 100			
11.	50 to 100			
12.	35 to 100			
13.	66 to 100			
14.	75 to 100			
15.	15 to 100			

	Ratio	Fraction	Decimal	Percent
16.	9 to 100			
17.	80 to 100			
18.	21 to 100			
19.	1 to 100			
20.	99 to 100			
21.	100 to 100			
22.	84 to 100			

Percents and Fractions

Write the lowest-terms fraction for each percent.

1. 40% _____   **2.** 30% _____   **3.** 55% _____

4. 64% _____   **5.** 36% _____   **6.** 25% _____

7. 2% _____   **8.** 80% _____   **9.** 44% _____

10. 60% _____   **11.** 12% _____   **12.** 85% _____

13. 72% _____   **14.** 96% _____   **15.** 8% _____

Write each fraction as a percent.

16. $\frac{1}{10}$ _____   **17.** $\frac{3}{20}$ _____   **18.** $\frac{33}{50}$ _____

19. $\frac{3}{4}$ _____   **20.** $\frac{13}{100}$ _____   **21.** $\frac{1}{5}$ _____

22. $\frac{1}{100}$ _____   **23.** $\frac{12}{25}$ _____   **24.** $\frac{7}{10}$ _____

25. $\frac{9}{25}$ _____   **26.** $\frac{11}{20}$ _____   **27.** $\frac{1}{2}$ _____

28. $\frac{1}{4}$ _____   **29.** $\frac{9}{10}$ _____   **30.** $\frac{3}{5}$ _____

Write each fraction in the lowest terms.
Then write a percent for the fraction.

31. $\frac{16}{32}$ _____ _____   **32.** $\frac{9}{90}$ _____ _____   **33.** $\frac{21}{30}$ _____ _____

34. $\frac{27}{45}$ _____ _____   **35.** $\frac{12}{40}$ _____ _____   **36.** $\frac{47}{100}$ _____ _____

37. $\frac{45}{60}$ _____ _____   **38.** $\frac{17}{100}$ _____ _____   **39.** $\frac{120}{160}$ _____ _____

40. $\frac{9}{30}$ _____ _____   **41.** $\frac{24}{12}$ _____ _____   **42.** $\frac{95}{100}$ _____ _____

Name _____

Percents and Decimals

Write each percent as a decimal.

1. 78% _____ **2.** 24% _____ **3.** 19% _____

4. 46% _____ **5.** 4% _____ **6.** 83% _____

7. 19% _____ **8.** 7% _____ **9.** 29% _____

10. 95% _____ **11.** 1% _____ **12.** 14% _____

13. 22.2% _____ **14.** 15.8% _____ **15.** 6.4% _____

16. 77.35% _____ **17.** 100% _____ **18.** 46.29% _____

19. 1.36% _____ **20.** 455% _____ **21.** 182% _____

22. 4.28% _____ **23.** 46.71% _____ **24.** 9.9% _____

Write each decimal as a percent.

25. 0.08 _____ **26.** 0.52 _____ **27.** 0.74 _____

28. 0.81 _____ **29.** 0.02 _____ **30.** 0.13 _____

31. 0.66 _____ **32.** 0.072 _____ **33.** 0.545 _____

34. 0.0017 _____ **35.** 0.1231 _____ **36.** 0.0626 _____

37. 0.015 _____ **38.** 1 _____ **39.** 0.0525 _____

40. 0.398 _____ **41.** 0.9 _____ **42.** 0.148 _____

43. 8.3 _____ **44.** 0.621 _____ **45.** 0.111 _____

46. 5 _____ **47.** 1.48 _____ **48.** 3.296 _____

Fractions, Decimals, and Percents

Use a calculator to find which is greater.

1. $\frac{1}{5}$ or 25% _____

2. 12% or $\frac{1}{8}$ _____

3. $\frac{1}{3}$ or 34% _____

4. 28.56% or $\frac{2}{7}$ _____

5. $\frac{2}{9}$ or 22.1% _____

6. 9% or $\frac{1}{11}$ _____

7. $\frac{7}{17}$ or 41.2% _____

8. 90.4% or $\frac{19}{21}$ _____

9. $\frac{4}{7}$ or 57% _____

10. 88.9% or $\frac{8}{9}$ _____

11. $\frac{5}{12}$ or 42% _____

12. 5% or $\frac{1}{2}$ _____

13. $\frac{9}{13}$ or 69% _____

14. 84% or $\frac{5}{6}$ _____

15. $\frac{3}{4}$ or 83.4% _____

16. 96.9% or $\frac{32}{33}$ _____

17. $\frac{3}{14}$ or 21% _____

18. 40% or $\frac{4}{9}$ _____

19. $\frac{5}{16}$ or 30% _____

20. 78% or $\frac{15}{19}$ _____

21. $\frac{3}{8}$ or 37% _____

22. 45% or $\frac{8}{18}$ _____

23. $\frac{3}{20}$ or 14% _____

24. 35% or $\frac{6}{15}$ _____

25. $\frac{1}{13}$ or 7.5% _____

26. 17% or $\frac{3}{18}$ _____

27. $\frac{5}{8}$ or 62% _____

Use mental math to find which is greater.

28. $\frac{9}{16}$ or 50% _____

29. 50% or $\frac{11}{24}$ _____

30. $\frac{6}{20}$ or 25% _____

31. 25% or $\frac{2}{12}$ _____

32. $\frac{10}{12}$ or 75% _____

33. 75% or $\frac{5}{8}$ _____

Functions and Function Notation

Evaluate each function for the value given.

1. Find $f(3)$ for $f(x) = x + 17$ _____

2. Find $f(6)$ for $f(j) = 3j - 4$ _____

3. Find $f(9)$ for $f(d) = 5d + 6$ _____

4. Find $f(1)$ for $f(k) = 10 - 8k$ _____

5. Find $f(2)$ for $f(r) = \dfrac{r + 12}{2}$ _____

6. Find $f(6)$ for $f(n) = \dfrac{n}{2} + 7$ _____

7. Find $f(4)$ for $f(a) =$ $(a - 1) \cdot (a + 2)$ _____

8. Find $f(9)$ for $f(p) =$ $(p - 5) \cdot (p + 4)$ _____

9. Find $f(0)$ for $f(w) = w(w + 3)$ _____

10. Find $f(10)$ for $f(z) = 5(z + 2)$ _____

11. Find $f(0.5)$ for $f(m) = 4m + 2$ _____

12. Find $f(4)$ for $f(y) = y^2 - 1$ _____

13. Find $f(10)$ for $f(t) = \dfrac{t^2 + 5}{15}$ _____

14. Find $f(15)$ for $f(g) = \dfrac{3q + 5}{10}$ _____

15. Find $f(\tfrac{1}{3})$ for $f(a) = 6 - 6a$ _____

16. Find $f(9)$ for $f(c) = 83 - c^2$ _____

17. Find $f(6)$ for $f(b) =$ $(b + 3) \cdot (b - 3)$ _____

18. Find $f(5)$ for $f(p) = 8p^2$ _____

Complete each table.

19. $f(x) = 7x + 6$

x	0	1	2	3	4	5	6	7	8	9	10
$f(x)$											

20. $f(y) = 100 - y^2$

y	0	1	2	3	4	5	6	7	8	9	10
$f(y)$											

Percents Greater Than 100 and Less Than 1

Using proportions, express each fraction as a
percent. Round to the nearest tenth of a percent.

1. $\frac{1}{175}$ _____

2. $\frac{9}{4}$ _____

3. $\frac{7}{5}$ _____

4. $\frac{3}{500}$ _____

5. $\frac{7}{800}$ _____

6. $\frac{15}{7}$ _____

7. $\frac{18}{5}$ _____

8. $\frac{3}{1,000}$ _____

9. $\frac{3}{400}$ _____

10. $\frac{9}{2}$ _____

11. $\frac{9}{8}$ _____

12. $\frac{21}{10}$ _____

13. $\frac{2}{725}$ _____

14. $\frac{5}{600}$ _____

Express each percent as a whole number, a
fraction, or a mixed number in lowest terms, and
as a decimal. Use a calculator.

15. 160% _____ _____

16. $\frac{5}{8}$% _____ _____

17. $\frac{3}{5}$% _____ _____

18. 420% _____ _____

19. 385% _____ _____

20. $\frac{7}{50}$% _____ _____

21. 1,000% _____ _____

22. $\frac{1}{4}$% _____ _____

23. $\frac{9}{10}$% _____ _____

24. 202% _____ _____

25. $\frac{13}{20}$% _____ _____

26. 135% _____ _____

27. 210% _____ _____

28. $\frac{4}{5}$% _____ _____

Name _____

Finding Percent Patterns

Use percent patterns to help you fill in the missing
data in the tables below.

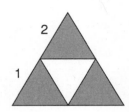

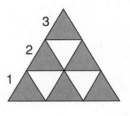

Number of Segments	Shaded Triangles	White Triangles	Total Triangles	Percent Shaded	Percent White
2	3	1	4	75	25
3	6	3	9	66.7	33.3
4	10	6	16	62.5	37.5
. . .	. . .	. . .	. . .	. . .	. . .
7	28	21	49	57.1	42.9
8	_____	_____	_____	_____	_____
9	_____	_____	_____	_____	_____
10	_____	_____	_____	_____	_____

In the pattern at the right, each shaded square is $\frac{1}{4}$
of the square that contains it.

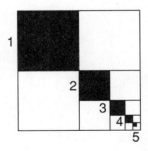

Shaded Square Number	Fraction of the Whole Square	Percent of the Whole Square
1	$\frac{1}{4}$	25
2	$\frac{1}{16}$	6.25
3	$\frac{1}{64}$	1.56
4	_____	_____
5	_____	_____

Fractional Percents

Complete the table.

	Percent as a Fraction	Percent as a Decimal	Decimal
1.	$16\frac{1}{2}\%$	_____	_____
2.	$1\frac{9}{25}\%$	_____	_____
3.	$8\frac{1}{4}\%$	_____	_____
4.	$100\frac{1}{2}\%$	_____	_____
5.	$21\frac{3}{20}\%$	_____	_____
6.	$45\frac{8}{10}\%$	_____	_____
7.	_____	_____	0.7325
8.	_____	_____	0.082
9.	_____	_____	0.9999
10.	_____	_____	1.034
11.	_____	_____	0.0488
12.	_____	_____	0.59125
13.	_____	63.64%	_____
14.	_____	8.1%	_____
15.	_____	16.22%	_____
16.	_____	33.875%	_____

Estimating Percents

Solve. Use estimation.

In Erin's writing class, 17 students speak only English at home and 12 students speak primarily Spanish at home. No one speaks any other languages.

1. About what percent of the class speaks only English at home?

_____

2. About what percent of the class speaks primarily Spanish at home?

_____

In Jumar's geography class, the teacher asked the students where they would like to live when they get older. Seven students said they would like to live in a suburb, 11 said in the city, and 16 said at the beach.

3. About what percent would like to live in a suburb?

_____

4. About what percent would like to live in the city?

_____

5. About what percent would like to live at the beach?

_____

Eight members of the track team competed in throwing events. Each person competed in only one event. 22 sprinted and 11 ran long distances.

6. About what percent of the track team competed in throwing events?

_____

7. About what percent of the track team competed in sprinting events?

_____

8. About what percent of the track team competed in long-distance runs?

_____

Using the Strategies

Solve. Use objects or act out.

1. In gym class, twice as many people wanted to play volleyball than wanted to play basketball. Six more people wanted to play basketball than wanted to do gymnastics. Seven people wanted to do gymnastics. How many people wanted to play volleyball?

2. Erin, Shannon, and Tara were sending out party invitations to all of their friends. Erin licked the envelopes, Shannon addressed them, and Tara stamped them. Each step took 5 seconds. How long did it take them to do the first six envelopes?

The items on sale this week at a school supply store are listed in the table.

Pens	box of 12	$2.50
Crayons	box of 8	$1.25
Paper	100 sheets	$1.80
Scissors	set of 2 pairs	$5.00

3. Marissa needs to buy 4 boxes of crayons, 200 sheets of paper, and 6 pairs of scissors for her art project. How much money will her supplies cost?

4. Angelo spent $12.60 on paper. How many sheets of paper did he buy?

5. If Verna spent $9.30 on paper and pens, how much of each of the two did she buy?

Name _____

Finding a Percent of a Number

Find the percent of each number.
Use a fraction for the percent. Show your work.

1. 50% of 70 = _____

2. 80% of 40 = _____

3. 10% of 60 = _____

_____   _____   _____

4. 40% of 35 = _____

5. 25% of 44 = _____

6. 90% of 50 = _____

_____   _____   _____

Find the percent of each number.
Use a decimal for the percent. Show your work.

7. 14% of 50 = _____

8. 86% of 200 = _____

9. 20% of 66 = _____

_____   _____   _____

10. 40% of 111 = _____

11. 8% of 10 = _____

12. 107% of 120 = _____

_____   _____   _____

Use mental math to find 10% of each number.

13. 10% of 36 = _____

14. 10% of 286 = _____

15. 10% of 24 = _____

16. 10% of 300 = _____

17. 10% of 7 = _____

18. 10% of 85 = _____

Use mental math to find 1% of each number.

19. 1% of 44 = _____

20. 1% of 9,000 = _____

21. 1% of 160 = _____

22. 1% of 15 = _____

23. 1% of 60 = _____

24. 1% of 900 = _____

25. 7% of 50 is what number? _____

26. 7% of 200 is what number? _____

Estimating a Percent of a Number

Use compatible numbers to estimate.

1. 68% of 52 _____

2. 9% of 145 _____

3. 39.4% of 25 _____

4. 74% of 48 _____

5. 19% of 72 _____

6. 48% of 70 _____

7. 74% of 100 _____

8. 34% of 69 _____

9. 18% of 40 _____

10. 79% of 46 _____

11. 12% of 52 _____

12. $8\frac{1}{2}$% of 24 _____

13. 26% of 88 _____

14. 62% of 300 _____

15. 48% of 4,000 _____

16. 49.5% of 10 _____

17. $9\frac{1}{2}$% of 200 _____

18. 32% of 50 _____

19. 21% of 420 _____

20. 11% of 196 _____

21. About how much is 14% of 70? _____

22. About how much is 10.9% of 420? _____

23. About how much is 74% of 32? _____

24. About how much is 57% of 90? _____

25. About how much is $48\frac{1}{2}$% of 48? _____

26. About how much is 37.2% of 120? _____

Finding Simple Interest

Use your calculator and the formula $I = PRT$ to find the interest.

1. $P = \$2,000$
$R = 10\%$ per year
$T = 3$ years

$I = $ _____

2. $P = \$15,000$
$R = 14\%$ per year
$T = 4$ months

$I = $ _____

3. $P = \$4,250$
$R = 1.5\%$ per month
$T = 7$ months

$I = $ _____

4. $P = \$720$
$R = 12\%$ per year
$T = 1.5$ years

$I = $ _____

5. $P = \$980$
$R = 8\%$ per year
$T = 6$ months

$I = $ _____

6. $P = \$1,250$
$R = 18\%$ per year
$T = 3$ months

$I = $ _____

7. $P = \$7,000$
$R = 15\%$ per year
$T = 3.5$ years

$I = $ _____

8. $P = \$1,600$
$R = 1.6\%$ per month
$T = 5$ months

$I = $ _____

9. $P = \$3,400$
$R = 9.5\%$ per year
$T = 2$ years

$I = $ _____

Use your calculator to find the interest I and the amount A.

10. $P = \$500$
$R = 5\%$ per year
$T = 2$ years

$I = $ _____

$A = $ _____

11. $P = \$1,000$
$R = 8\%$ per year
$T = 3$ years

$I = $ _____

$A = $ _____

12. $P = \$2,500$
$R = 6\%$ per year
$T = 10$ years

$I = $ _____

$A = $ _____

13. $P = \$1,500$
$R = 9\%$ per year
$T = 2$ years

$I = $ _____

$A = $ _____

14. $P = \$1,800$
$R = 12\%$ per year
$T = 5$ years

$I = $ _____

$A = $ _____

15. $P = \$2,000$
$R = 8.5\%$ per year
$T = 1$ year

$I = $ _____

$A = $ _____

Applying Percent: Finding the Percent One Number Is of Another

Solve. Round to the nearest whole percent.

1. 69 is what percent of 99? _____

2. What percent of 8 is 6? _____

3. What percent of 15 is 12? _____

4. 13 is what percent of 52? _____

5. 10 is what percent of 13? _____

6. What percent of 48 is 18? _____

7. What percent of 11 is 4? _____

8. 35 is what percent of 49? _____

9. What percent of 250 is 75? _____

10. What percent of 4 is 1? _____

11. 72 is what percent of 90? _____

12. 11 is what percent of 19? _____

13. What percent of 5 is 2? _____

14. 30 is what percent of 30? _____

15. What percent of 125 is 25? _____

16. What percent of 90 is 18? _____

17. 7 is what percent of 8? _____

18. 49 is what percent of 50? _____

19. What percent of 9 is 6? _____

20. 6 is what percent of 10? _____

21. 10 is what percent of 14? _____

22. 3 is what percent of 20? _____

23. What percent of 40 is 12? _____

24. What percent of 60 is 48? _____

25. 20 is what percent of 80? _____

26. What percent of 60 is 9? _____

27. 9 is what percent of 10? _____

28. 18 is what percent of 72? _____

29. What percent of 10 is 20? _____

30. What percent of 96 is 60? _____

Percent of Increase or Decrease

Use your calculator to find the percent of increase
or decrease to the nearest percent.

1. 16 to 38 _____   **2.** 43 to 5 _____

3. 112 to 114 _____   **4.** 3 to 5 _____

5. 7 to 58 _____   **6.** 99 to 3 _____

Janet made this chart of her expenses in April and
May. Complete the chart.

	Expense	April	May	Increase or Decrease	Amount	Percent
7.	Travel	$ 40	$ 50	_____	_____	_____
8.	Food	225	189	_____	_____	_____
9.	Entertainment	45	99	_____	_____	_____
10.	Rent and Utilities	360	378	_____	_____	_____
11.	Clothing	155	62	_____	_____	_____
12.	Other	135	108	_____	_____	_____
13.	TOTAL	960	886	_____	_____	_____

Find the percent of increase or decrease.

14. Larry bought a television for $40. After making
some repairs, he sold the television for $70. _____

15. The average temperature in August was 90°F.
The average temperature in September was 75°F. _____

16. Irma scored 6 points in the first half of the
basketball game. She scored 15 points in the
second half of the game. _____

Using Critical Thinking

Solve. Use a calculator.

1. A 16-oz box of cereal that sells for $2.20 is now 25% off. A different type of cereal contains 25% more cereal and sells for $2.20. Which box of cereal is the better buy?

_____

2. Bottle A contains 36 oz of apple juice for $1.59. It is now on sale for 20% off. Bottle B contains 25% more and sells for $1.99. Which bottle has the lower cost per ounce? To the nearest cent, how much less is the cost per ounce for this bottle?

_____

3. A 10-oz bar of cheese that originally sold for $1.89 is now 10% off. A second bar of cheese has 20% more cheese than the 10-oz bar. Set a price for the second bar so that neither of the bars of cheese is a better buy than the other.

_____

4. An 18-oz jar of peanut butter costs $2.20. The peanut butter is now on sale for 25% off. A second jar of peanut butter has 25% more than the first and sells for $2.90. Which is the better buy?

_____

5. A $9,000 car is on sale for 20% off. A $12,000 car is on sale for 35% off. Which car will cost less money to buy? How much less?

_____

6. A $28 pair of shoes is on sale for 20% off. A $32 pair of shoes is also on sale. Set the percent off the second pair so the shoes cost the same price.

_____

7. Box A of cereal contains 15 oz and sells for $2.60. Box A is now on sale for 15% off. Box B contains 10% more than Box A and sells for $2.60. Which box is the better buy? To the nearest cent, how much less is the cost per ounce of this box?

_____

8. A 12-oz can of juice sells for $0.89. It is now on sale for 10% off. A second can contains 50% more and sells for $1. Which is the better buy?

_____

Applying Percent: Finding a Number from a Percent

Solve each equation.

1. $30\% \times n = 18$ $n =$ _____

2. $25\% \times n = 10$ $n =$ _____

3. $8\% \times n = 32$ $n =$ _____

4. $45\% \times n = 54$ $n =$ _____

5. $3\% \times n = 1.5$ $n =$ _____

6. $12\% \times n = 0.96$ $n =$ _____

7. $33\% \times n = 21.45$ $n =$ _____

8. $49\% \times n = 9.8$ $n =$ _____

Write and solve an equation for each problem.

9. 40% of what number is 30?

10. 6% of what number is 15?

11. 25% of what number is 11?

12. 96% of what number is 24?

13. 8% of what number is 1.2?

14. 10% of what number is 4.6?

15. 67% of what number is 26.8?

16. 52% of what number is 33.8?

Discount and Sale Prices

Find the amount of the discount and the sale price.
Use a calculator.

1. Regular Price: $52
    Discount Percent: 25%

    Discount: _____

    Sale Price: _____

2. Regular Price: $90
    Discount Percent: 15%

    Discount: _____

    Sale Price: _____

3. Regular Price: $80
    Discount Percent: 20%

    Discount: _____

    Sale Price: _____

4. Regular Price: $1,200
    Discount Percent: 12%

    Discount: _____

    Sale Price: _____

5. Regular Price: $36.50
    Discount Percent: 40%

    Discount: _____

    Sale Price: _____

6. Regular Price: $70
    Discount Percent: 30%

    Discount: _____

    Sale Price: _____

7. Regular Price: $17.80
    Discount Percent: 10%

    Discount: _____

    Sale Price: _____

8. Regular Price: $120
    Discount Percent: 15%

    Discount: _____

    Sale Price: _____

9. Regular Price: $250
    Discount Percent: 18%

    Discount: _____

    Sale Price: _____

10. Regular Price: $16.50
    Discount Percent: 50%

    Discount: _____

    Sale Price: _____

Making Circle Graphs

Use the data from each survey to make a circle graph. Use a
calculator to find the number of degrees in each central angle.
Round to the nearest degree.

1. What is your favorite type of movie?

Comedy	46%
Drama	17%
Action and Adventure	25%
Documentary	12%

2. What is your favorite type of book?

Romance	22%
Mystery	37%
Nonfiction	18%
Autobiography	15%
Biography	8%

3. What is your favorite sport?

Baseball	32%
Basketball	22%
Football	37.5%
Hockey	3.5%
Soccer	5%

4. What is your favorite season?

Winter	6%
Spring	52%
Summer	14%
Fall	28%

Exploring Algebra: Solving Percent Problems

Translate to an equation and solve.

1. What number is 40% of 90? _____

2. What percent of 500 is 75? _____

3. 42 is 70% of what number? _____

4. 27 out of 30 is what percent? _____

5. 45% of 500 is what number? _____

6. 102 is 85% of what number _____

7. 12 out of 15 is what percent? _____

8. 30% of 60 is what number? _____

9. 70% of 120 is what number? _____

10. 17 is 25% of what number? _____

11. 125% of 80 is what number? _____

12. What percent is 13 of 65? _____

13. 21 out of 300 is what percent? _____

14. What percent is 22 of 88? _____

Use mental math to solve for n.

15. 50% of $n = 20$ _____   **16.** 10% of $n = 67$ _____

17. 40 out of 80 $= n\%$ _____   **18.** 40 out of 50 $= n\%$ _____

19. 1% of $20 = n$ _____   **20.** 25% of $100 = n$ _____

21. 12 out of 48 $= n\%$ _____   **22.** 150% of $90 = n$ _____

23. 90 out of 200 is $n\%$ _____   **24.** 20% of $n = 24$ _____

Problems Without Solutions

Solve. If there is no solution, tell why.

1. Nick is putting a new tile floor in his kitchen. The length of the kitchen is 18 feet. If each tile is 3 feet long, how many tiles will fit in the length of the kitchen?

_____

_____

2. Three-foot-long tiles cost $8.75 each. Nick gave the store clerk $350 to pay for 36 tiles plus the tax. What was his change?

_____

_____

3. Kathleen gave a clerk 6 coins to buy a card that cost $0.80. She did not receive any change. What coins did she use?

_____

_____

4. Ethan read a 4-page article on race cars. He noticed that the page numbers added up to 62. On what page did the article begin?

_____

_____

5. Amanda planted the same number of rows of corn, peppers, and tomatoes in her garden. The garden has 26 rows of plants. How many rows of each are in Amanda's garden?

_____

_____

6. A triangle is inscribed in a rectangle. Both share a 4-cm-long side. The vertex of the triangle opposite the 4-cm-long side touches the opposite side of the rectangle. The area of the triangle is 8 cm^2. Is the rectangle a square?

_____

_____

7. Admission to the town pool is $1.25 for adults and $0.75 for children. Mrs. Costa purchased 5 tickets. She gave the cashier $5 and received $0.25 in change. What tickets did she buy?

_____

_____

8. The next time Mrs. Costa visited the pool, she purchased 8 tickets. She gave the cashier $10 and received $3 change. What tickets did she buy?

_____

_____

Understanding Integers

Write the opposite for each integer.

1. $^+3$ _____   **2.** $^-5$ _____   **3.** $^-7$ _____   **4** $^+9$ _____

5. $^-6$ _____   **6.** 0 _____   **7.** $^+4$ _____   **8.** $^-1$ _____

9. $^-8$ _____   **10.** $^+2$ _____   **11.** $^+15$ _____   **12.** $^-13$ _____

Use the number line to compare the integers.
Write > or < for each $\bigcirc$.

13. $^+8 \bigcirc ^-6$ **14.** $^-7 \bigcirc ^-4$ **15.** $^-9 \bigcirc ^+5$

16. $^+7 \bigcirc ^+2$ **17.** $^+3 \bigcirc ^-5$ **18.** $^+1 \bigcirc ^-1$

19. $^-7 \bigcirc ^+3$ **20.** $^-2 \bigcirc 0$ **21.** $0 \bigcirc ^+4$

22. $^+9 \bigcirc ^-4$ **23.** $^-7 \bigcirc ^-3$ **24.** $^+2 \bigcirc ^-1$

For each situation, give the suggested integer and
its opposite.

25. $10 reduction _____   **26.** an elevation of 5 feet _____

27. lose 1 hour's sleep _____   **28.** dig down 3 feet _____

Properties of Integers

Use the opposites property to find the missing integers.

1. $^+6 + {}^-6 = $ _____

2. _____ $+ {}^-3 = 0$

3. $^-4 + $ _____ $= 0$

4. $^-21 + $ _____ $= 0$

5. $^+17 + {}^-17 = $ _____

6. $^+8 + {}^-8 = $ _____

Use the zero or the one property to find the missing integers.

7. $^+8 + 0 = $ _____

8. $^-7 + 0 = $ _____

9. $^+9 \cdot $ _____ $= {}^+9$

10. $^-3 \cdot {}^+1 = $ _____

11. $^+16 + $ _____ $= {}^+16$

12. $^+11 \cdot $ _____ $= {}^+11$

Use the commutative properties to write the addends or factors in a different way.

13. $^+4 \cdot {}^+2$ _____

14. $^-5 + {}^+10$ _____

15. $^+8 + {}^+9$ _____

16. $^+12 \cdot {}^-3$ _____

Use the associative property to write the addends or factors in a different way.

17. $(^+5 + {}^+2) + {}^+3$ _____

18. $^-8 + (^-8 + {}^+3)$ _____

19. $^+6 \cdot (^+8 \cdot {}^+4)$ _____

20. $(^+12 \cdot {}^-3) \cdot {}^+2$ _____

Use the distributive property to write the addends or factors in a different way.

21. $^+3 \cdot (^+4 + {}^+6)$ _____

22. $(^+2 \cdot {}^+5) + (^+2 \cdot {}^-3)$ _____

23. $^-6 \cdot (^+8 + {}^+3)$ _____

24. $(^-7 \cdot {}^-8) + (^-7 \cdot {}^-2)$ _____

Adding Integers

Use white chips as positive integers and red chips as
negative integers. For each example, write the value of Set A
and Set B and of the combined set. Then write an equation.

	Set A	Set B	Combined Set	Equation
1.	○○○	●●	○○○ / ●●	
2.	●●●	○○	●●● / ○○	
3.	○○	●●●	○○ / ●●●	
4.	●●	○○○	●● / ○○○	

Write equations for Exercises 5–9.

5. Use both positive and negative chips. Write equations

that represent $^-3$ in two different ways. _____

6. Write equations that represent $^+1$ in two different ways. _____

7. Write equations that represent 0 in two different ways. _____

8. Combine a set of 3 whites and 5 reds with another

set to represent 0. _____

9. Combine a set of 4 whites and 1 red with another set

to represent 0. _____

Find the sums. Use chips if necessary.

10. $^-3 + {}^-6$ = _____   **11.** $^-7 + {}^+11$ = _____   **12.** $^-2 + {}^+9$ = _____

13. $^+12 + {}^-8$ = _____   **14.** $^+14 + {}^-5$ = _____   **15.** $^-3 + {}^+8$ = _____

16. $^-7 + {}^-7$ = _____   **17.** $^+12 + {}^-12$ = _____   **18.** $^+13 + {}^-5$ = _____

Subtracting Integers

Use white chips for positive integers and red chips for
negative integers. For each exercise, find the remaining
set when Set B is removed from Set A. Write an equation
that represents the subtraction.

	Set A	Set B	Remaining Set	Equation
1.	0	⁻4		
2.	0	4		
3.	⁻4	0		
4.	4	0		
5.	9	⁻3		
6.	⁻9	⁻3		
7.	9	3		
8.	⁻9	3		

Write **true** or **false** for each statement. If a statement is
false, give an example to prove it.

9. If a positive number is subtracted from
a positive number, the result is always
positive.

_____

10. If a negative number is subtracted
from a negative number, the result is
always negative.

_____

11. If zero is subtracted from an integer,
the result is the integer.

_____

12. If a number is subtracted from its
opposite, the result is always zero.

_____

Subtract.

13. $12 - {}^-3 =$ _____

14. $13 - 17 =$ _____

15. $7 - {}^-9 =$ _____

16. ${}^-8 - 15 =$ _____

17. ${}^-20 - 15 =$ _____

18. $3 - {}^-6 =$ _____

Evaluate each expression. Compute inside parentheses first.

19. $6 + ({}^-5 - {}^-3) =$ _____

20. ${}^-5 - ({}^-11 - 6) =$ _____

Integer Multiplication Patterns

Complete the tables. Look for multiplication patterns.

	Product	Difference
2×3 =	6	
		$^-2$
2×2 =	4	
2×1 =	_____	_____
2×0 =	_____	_____
$2 \times ^-1$ =	_____	_____
$2 \times ^-2$ =	_____	_____
$2 \times ^-3$ =	_____	_____

	Product	Difference
$^-3 \times 3$ =	_____	
$^-3 \times 2$ =	_____	_____
$^-3 \times 1$ =	_____	_____
$^-3 \times 0$ =	_____	_____
$^-3 \times ^-1$ =	_____	_____
$^-3 \times ^-2$ =	_____	_____
$^-3 \times ^-3$ =	_____	_____

Complete the multiplications. Look for patterns.

$2 \times 1 =$ _____ $2 \times ^-1 =$ _____ $1 \times ^-3 =$ _____ $^-1 \times ^-3 =$ _____

$2 \times 2 =$ _____ $2 \times ^-2 =$ _____ $2 \times ^-3 =$ _____ $^-2 \times ^-3 =$ _____

$2 \times 3 =$ _____ $2 \times ^-3 =$ _____ $3 \times ^-3 =$ _____ $^-3 \times ^-3 =$ _____

What pattern do you see in the products of two positive integers as opposed to the products of one negative and one positive integer?

_____

_____

_____

_____

What pattern do you see in the products of one positive integer and one negative integer as opposed to the products of two negative integers?

_____

_____

_____

_____

Multiplying Integers

Multiply.

1. $^-5 \cdot 7$ _____

2. $^-10 \cdot 7$ _____

3. $^-8 \cdot ^-4$ _____

4. $^-9 \cdot ^-6$ _____

5. $^-8 \cdot 11$ _____

6. $3 \cdot ^-7$ _____

7. $5 \cdot ^-10$ _____

8. $^-12 \cdot 4$ _____

9. $^-16 \cdot ^-2$ _____

10. $^-8 \cdot ^-3$ _____

11. $^-7 \cdot ^-10$ _____

12. $^-30 \cdot ^-4$ _____

13. $^-4 \cdot 7$ _____

14. $15 \cdot ^-3$ _____

15. $^-9 \cdot 6$ _____

16. $^-8 \cdot 9$ _____

17. $^-2 \cdot ^-6$ _____

18. $^-9 \cdot ^-4$ _____

19. $^-6 \cdot 4$ _____

20. $6 \cdot ^-17$ _____

21. $8 \cdot ^-6$ _____

22. $3 \cdot ^-12$ _____

23. $^-5 \cdot 4$ _____

24. $^-13 \cdot ^-1$ _____

25. $6 \cdot ^-10$ _____

26. $^-3 \cdot 8$ _____

27. $13 \cdot ^-2$ _____

28. $7 \cdot ^-8$ _____

29. $^-2 \cdot ^-21$ _____

30. $^-1 \cdot 32$ _____

31. $9 \cdot ^-6$ _____

32. $^-3 \cdot ^-15$ _____

33. $^-11 \cdot ^-3$ _____

34. $^-13 \cdot 0$ _____

35. $^-5 \cdot ^-10$ _____

36. $^-2 \cdot 16$ _____

Evaluate each expression.

37. $(^-3 \cdot 4) \cdot ^-3$ _____

38. $^-5 \cdot (^-2 \cdot ^-6)$ _____

39. $(7 \cdot ^-3) \cdot ^-4$ _____

40. $9 \cdot (^-4 \cdot ^-1)$ _____

41. $^-6 \cdot (^-5 \cdot 6)$ _____

42. $(^-8 \cdot ^-3) \cdot 2$ _____

43. $6 \cdot (3 + ^-4)$ _____

44. $(^-5 \cdot 3) + (^-5 \cdot ^-6)$ _____

45. $(^-3 \cdot ^-4) - 3$ _____

46. $(4 \cdot 8) + (2 \cdot ^-3)$ _____

Dividing Integers

Use the given multiplication fact to find the related quotients.

1. $^-6 \cdot 3 = {}^-18$

$^-18 \div {}^-6 =$ _____

$^-18 \div 3 \ =$ _____

2. $^-9 \cdot 8 = {}^-72$

$^-72 \div {}^-9 =$ _____

$^-72 \div 8 \ =$ _____

3. $^-12 \cdot {}^-5 = 60$

$60 \div {}^-12 \ =$ _____

$60 \div {}^-5 \ \ =$ _____

Use multiplication to decide if each equation is correct. Write **yes** or **no**. If no, give the correct answer.

4. $^-52 \div 4 \ = {}^-13$ _____

5. $^-60 \div {}^-5 \ = {}^-12$ _____

6. $119 \div {}^-17 = {}^-7$ _____

7. $55 \div {}^-11 \ = {}^-5$ _____

8. $36 \div {}^-4 \ = 9$ _____

9. $^-60 \div {}^-4 \ = {}^-15$ _____

10. $^-48 \div {}^-6 \ = 8$ _____

11. $^-81 \div {}^-9 \ = 9$ _____

12. $^-126 \div 9 \ = {}^-14$ _____

Find the quotients.

13. $^-32 \div 4 \ =$ _____

14. $42 \div {}^-6 \ =$ _____

15. $^-105 \div 15 \ =$ _____

16. $^-48 \div 6 \ =$ _____

17. $^-20 \div {}^-5 \ =$ _____

18. $^-96 \div {}^-16 \ =$ _____

19. $^-56 \div 7 \ =$ _____

20. $^-35 \div {}^-7 \ =$ _____

21. $^-84 \div 12 \ =$ _____

22. $0 \div {}^-8 \ =$ _____

23. $^-54 \div {}^-6 \ =$ _____

24. $63 \div {}^-7 \ =$ _____

25. $27 \div {}^-9 \ =$ _____

26. $^-65 \div {}^-13 \ =$ _____

27. $81 \div {}^-3 \ =$ _____

28. $100 \div {}^-5 \ =$ _____

29. $^-64 \div {}^-4 \ =$ _____

30. $^-108 \div 12 \ =$ _____

31. $^-66 \div {}^-11 \ =$ _____

32. $125 \div {}^-25 \ =$ _____

33. $^-17 \div 17 \ =$ _____

34. $\dfrac{^-72}{-4} \ =$ _____

35. $\dfrac{^-51}{-3} \ =$ _____

36. $\dfrac{^-76}{-4} \ =$ _____

37. Divide $^-12$ by the opposite of 4.

_____

38. Divide 18 by the opposite of $^-6$.

_____

Graphing Integer Coordinates

Graph the points. Then connect the points to draw polygons.

1. ($^-$7, 6), ($^-$7, 7), (5, 6), (5, 7)

2. (1, $^-$1), (5, 3), ($^-$1, 5)

3. ($^-$1, $^-$1), ($^-$3, 1), ($^-$5, 1),
   ($^-$7, $^-$1), ($^-$5, $^-$2), ($^-$3, $^-$2)

4. ($^-$1, $^-$3), ($^-$5, $^-$6), (3, $^-$6),
   (6, $^-$3)

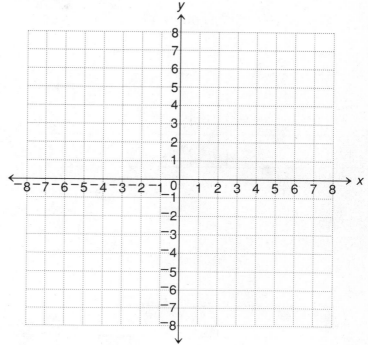

5. ($^-$3, 4), ($^-$1, 7), (3, 7), (5, 4)

6. (1, 1), (3, 3), (5, 3), (7, 1),
   (7, $^-$1), (5, $^-$3), (3, $^-$3), (1, $^-$1)

7. ($^-$2, 2), ($^-$2, $^-$2), ($^-$6, $^-$2),
   ($^-$6, 2)

8. ($^-$3, $^-$6), (4, $^-$4), (4, $^-$7)

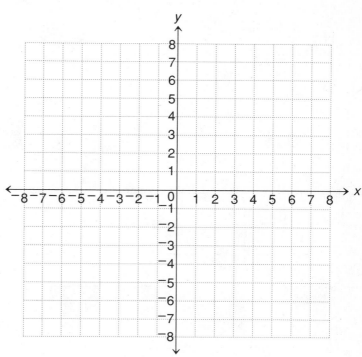

Exploring Algebra:
Graphing Equations

Complete each table. Then graph each equation.

Equation: $y = 1 - x$

x	4	2	0	$^-1$	$^-3$	$^-4$
y	$^-3$	$^-1$	1	2	4	5
(x, y)						

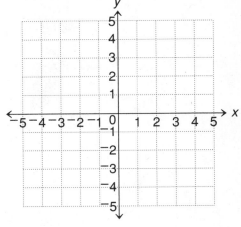

Equation: $y = \frac{1}{2}x + 1$

x	$^-4$	$^-2$	0	2	4
y	$^-1$	0	1	2	3
(x, y)					

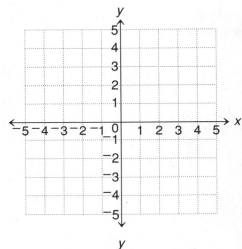

Equation: $y = x - 1$

x	5	3	1	$^-1$	$^-3$	$^-4$
y	4	2	0	$^-2$	$^-4$	$^-5$
(x, y)						

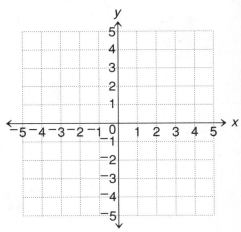

Using the Strategies

Solve. Some problems have more than one answer.

1. Eric and Shane are trying to find a night to go bowling in the month of September. Eric is off from work every Sunday, Monday, and Thursday night. Shane is off every third night. Today is Tuesday, September 1, and Shane is not working. What nights in September will they be able to go bowling?

_____

2. Mario and Nadine play in a round-robin tennis group. Mario plays every fourth day, while Nadine plays two days in a row and sits out the third day. On August 2 Mario played, but Nadine did not. On what days in August will Mario and Nadine both play?

_____

3. Derek went to the store and bought $0.90 worth of raisins. He handed the cashier $1.00 and the cashier gave him his change. What different coin combinations could the cashier have given him?

_____

4. Dina and Miguel were involved in a cooperative computer project that started at 9:00 a.m. Every 20 minutes, Dina would get a 10-minute break. Every 10 minutes, Miguel would get a 5-minute break. These cycles continued until 11:00 a.m. During what time periods were both Miguel and Dina on break?

_____

Name _____

Chance Events

The line at the right can be used to picture the
likelihood of an event occurring. Examine each exercise.
Decide where each event should be shown on the line.

Impossible ├─┼─┼─┼─┼─┼─┤ Certain
          A B C D E F G H

Exercises 1 to 6 refer to the spinner.

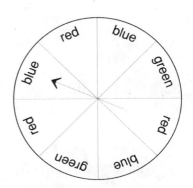

1. Spinning blue. _____

2. Spinning green. _____

3. Spinning red. _____

4. Spinning blue or red. _____

5. Spinning yellow. _____

6. Spinning red, blue, or green. _____

Exercises 7 to 10 refer to the number cube. Its
faces are numbered 1 to 6.

7. Throwing a 5 on the cube. _____

8. Throwing a number less than 5. _____

9. Throwing an even number. _____

10. Throwing a 1 or a 2. _____

Problems 11 and 12 are based on a toss of a
normalcoin.

11. Suppose you toss a coin 10 times.
Where on the line would you place
getting all tails?

    _____

12. Suppose you toss a coin 10 times.
Where on the line would you place
getting 5 tails?

    _____

Name _____

Sample Spaces

Consider a normal coin and a cube with numbers 1 to 6 on its faces. If the coin and cube are tossed at the same time, give the outcomes that make up each event.

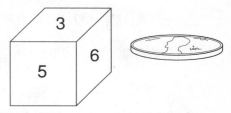

1. A 3 and a head

_____

2. A number greater than 3 and a tail

_____

3. An even number and a head

_____

4. A prime number and a tail

_____

A card is drawn from the hat at the same time that the spinner is spun. List the sample space of all the outcomes for the events that follow.

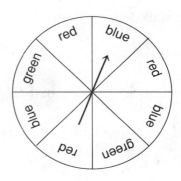

5. What outcomes make the event of getting a square number and a blue sector?

_____

_____

6. What outcomes make the event of getting a multiple of 3 and a blue or red?

_____

_____

A cube with numbers 1 to 6 on its faces is tossed at the same time that a number card is drawn from the hat above.

7. What outcomes make the event of getting a sum of 6 from the card and the cube?

_____

_____

8. What outcomes make the event of getting the same number on the card and on the cube?

_____

_____

Name _____

Probability of an Event

Use the spinner. Write the probability of each event.

1. $P(1)$ _____   **2.** $P(3)$ _____

3. $P(5)$ _____   **4.** $P(7)$ _____

5. $P(9)$ _____   **6.** $P(4)$ _____

7. P(an odd number) _____

8. P(an even number) _____

9. P(a prime number) _____

10. P(a number less than 6) _____

11. P(a number greater than 6) _____

12. P(a number greater than 10) _____

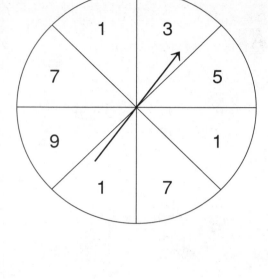

Think of dropping a disk onto the board. Write the probability of each event.

13. $P(1)$ _____   **14.** $P(3)$ _____

15. $P(6)$ _____   **16.** $P(10)$ _____

17. $P(8)$ _____   **18.** $P(2)$ _____

19. P(an odd number) _____

20. P(an even number) _____

21. P(a number less than 7) _____

22. P(a number greater than 10) _____

23. P(a prime number) _____

24. P(a number divisible by 3) _____

Name _____

Probability Experiments

Find the experimental probability of each event.

1. A coin is tossed. The tosses result in 24 heads, 16 tails.

   Exp P (heads) = _____

   Exp P (tails) = _____

2. Two number cubes are tossed 35 times. A sum of 8 appears 14 times.

   Exp P (sum of 8) = _____

3. Of the 3 choices for lunch, 15 students ate pizza, 3 students ate burgers, and 6 students ate sandwiches. What is the probability that the next student will select a burger?

   Exp P (burger) = _____

4. A spinner is spun 11 times. It lands on the number 5 three times, on the number 3 five times, and on the number 4 three times.

   Exp P (odd number) = _____

5. A spinner lands on red 5 times, on green 9 times, and on blue 4 times.

   Exp P (green) = _____

   Exp P (red) = _____

   Exp P (blue) = _____

6. In 20 draws of marbles from a box, 6 blue marbles are drawn and 4 red marbles are drawn.

   Exp P (blue) = _____

   Exp P (red) = _____

7. Refer to the table below. The mathematical probability in a coin-tossing experiment is $\frac{1}{2}$ or 0.5. Use a calculator to determine the experimental probability of tails for each student. Round to the nearest thousandth.

   Laurie _____

   Drew _____

   Juan _____

Laurie:	190 tails in 389 tosses
Drew:	281 tails in 550 tosses
Juan:	198 tails in 420 tosses

   Who had the experimental probability closest to

   the mathematical probability? _____

Using Critical Thinking: Analyzing and Testing Formulas

The formula and the experiment below it are related.
Answer the questions.

1. What is the purpose of the experiment?

_____

_____

_____

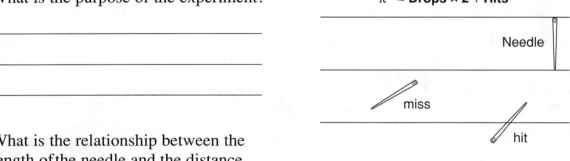

$\pi \approx$ **Drops × 2 ÷ Hits**

Needle

miss

hit

2. What is the relationship between the
length of the needle and the distance
between the lines?

_____

_____

3. Describe what is meant by a "hit."

_____

_____

_____

HITS	MISSES
|||| ||||	|||| |||

Does it count if the needle
hits the line and bounces off? _____

4. Do the experiment shown above using a toothpick
and paper with proportionately spaced lines. Drop
the toothpick 50 times and tally your results.

Is the result close to 3.14? _____

If not, how far away was your result? _____

5. Compare your tally at 30 drops with your tally at
50 drops. At which frequency are you closer to
3.14 as the value of π? _____

Exploring Algebra: Inequalities

Write an inequality for each statement.

1. Price p is greater than $2.98.

2. Height h is less than 52 inches.

3. Time t is less than 51 minutes.

4. Cost c will be at least $200.

5. Age a is at most 16.

6. Ratio r is greater than 3/5.

Write inequalities for these graphs.

7.

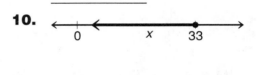

0   25 x

_____

8.

0   y 41

_____

9.

0 $2\frac{1}{2}$ y

_____

10.

0   x 33

_____

Draw graphs for these inequalities.

11. $x \leq 25$

12. $y > 5$

13. $m \geq 35$

14. $c < 26$

Answer each question **always**, **sometimes**, or **never**.

15. If $x \leq 7$, is $x < 7$?

16. If $x \geq 47$, is $x = 47$?

17. If $x > 23$, is $x < 18.5$?

Name _____

Tree Diagrams and Compound Events

Refer to the spinner below for Exercises 1 and 2.

$P(G) = \frac{1}{3}$

$P(Y) = \frac{1}{3}$

$P(B) = \frac{1}{3}$

1. Complete the tree diagram below.

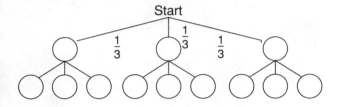

2. Make a sample space from the tree diagram in Exercise 1.

(____ , ____), (____ , ____), (____ , ____)

(____ , ____), (____ , ____), (____ , ____)

(____ , ____), (____ , ____), (____ , ____)

Use the tree diagram below to give the following answers.

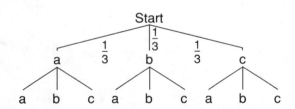

$P(a) = \frac{1}{3}$

$P(b) = \frac{1}{3}$

$P(c) = \frac{1}{3}$

3. P (2 letters the same)

_____

4. P (2 letters different)

_____

5. P (2 letters consonants)

_____

6. P (2 letters vowels)

_____

Use the tree diagram below to give the following answers.

7. P (R, R) = _____

8. P (A, A) = _____

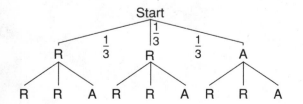

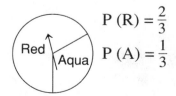

$P(R) = \frac{2}{3}$

$P(A) = \frac{1}{3}$

Use with text pages 354–355.

Name _____

Finding Related Problems

Read all the problems first and decide which are
related. Then solve each one.

1. Sue had $42 in her bank account. She put $7 in
each week for 19 weeks. She withdrew $14 for
a summer class she wanted to take. How much
money does she have left in her account?   _____

2. Layla has 7 sweatshirts. Four of them are large
and 3 are medium. If she chooses one, what is
the probability she will get a large sweatshirt?   _____

3. Jamie, Edith, Shanto, and Tom live in the same
4-story apartment house. Each lives on a
different floor. Jamie has the longest way up.
Tom doesn't take the elevator or the stairs.
Edith lives above Shanto, who prefers the stairs
to the elevator.
Where does each live?   _____

_____

_____

_____

4. Keith is beginning an exercise program. He
plans to walk 3 blocks the first week, 5 blocks
the second, 7 blocks the third week, and so on
until he walks 25 blocks regularly every week.
In which week will he first walk 25 blocks?   _____

5. Blair knows the first 3 numbers of Chad's
phone number and remembers that the last four
numbers are 5, 4, 7, and 8 but she does not
know the order. How many different
combinations might she have to try?   _____

Name _____

Expected Value

Find the expected value by making a table.
Exercise 1 has been started for you.

1.

Outcome	Number Expected in 150 spins	Total Points
2 points		
5 points	$\frac{1}{3}$ × 150 = 50	
7 points		
Total of All Spins		
Expected Value		

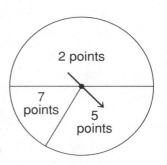

$P(2) = \frac{1}{2}$
$P(5) = \frac{1}{3}$
$P(7) = \frac{1}{6}$

Spin 150 times.

2.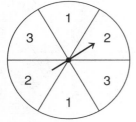

Spin 72 times.

Expected value _____

3.

Spin 40 times.

Expected value _____

4.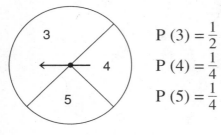

$P(3) = \frac{1}{2}$
$P(4) = \frac{1}{4}$
$P(5) = \frac{1}{4}$

Spin 40 times.

Expected value _____

5.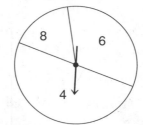

$P(4) = \frac{1}{2}$
$P(6) = \frac{1}{3}$
$P(8) = \frac{1}{6}$

Spin 36 times.

Expected value _____

Exploring the Concept of Area

Use the half-rectangle principle and the addition
principle to find the areas of these figures.

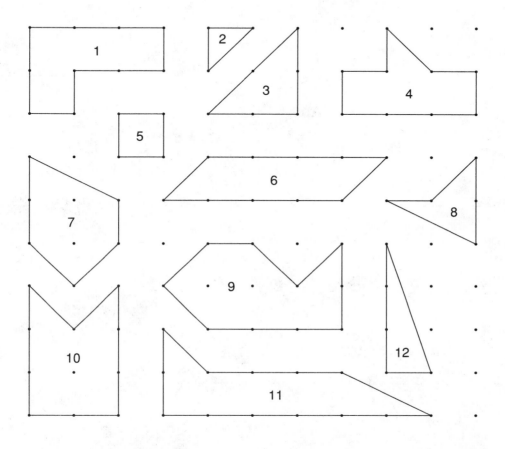

1. _____   **2.** _____   **3.** _____

4. _____   **5.** _____   **6.** _____

7. _____   **8.** _____   **9.** _____

10. _____   **11.** _____   **12.** _____

Area of Rectangles and Parallelograms

Find the area of each rectangle.

1.
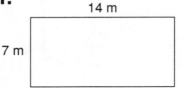
14 m

7 m

Area = _____

2.
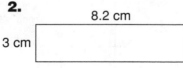
8.2 cm

3 cm

Area = _____

3.
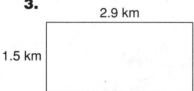
2.9 km

1.5 km

Area = _____

4. $l = 16$ cm
$w = 9$ cm

Area = _____

5. $l = 35$ m
$w = 10$ m

Area = _____

6. $l = 4.7$ m
$w = 3.0$ m

Area = _____

7. $l = 45$ mm
$w = 8$ mm

Area = _____

8. $l = 2.7$ cm
$w = 1.9$ cm

Area = _____

9. $l = 6.8$ m
$w = 0.8$ m

Area = _____

Find the area of each parallelogram.

10.
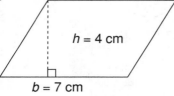
$h = 4$ cm

$b = 7$ cm

Area = _____

11.
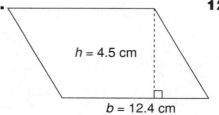
$h = 4.5$ cm

$b = 12.4$ cm

Area = _____

12.
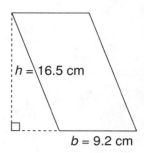
$h = 16.5$ cm

$b = 9.2$ cm

Area = _____

13. $b = 13$ cm
$h = 6$ cm

Area = _____

14. $b = 41$ cm
$h = 22$ cm

Area = _____

15. $b = 5.8$ m
$h = 4.0$ m

Area = _____

16. $b = 9.2$ cm
$h = 5.0$ cm

Area = _____

17. $b = 12.2$ m
$h = 3.5$ m

Area = _____

18. $b = 28$ m
$h = 14$ m

Area = _____

Name _____

Area of Triangles and Trapezoids

Use the formula $A = \frac{1}{2}bh$ to find the area of each triangle.

1.

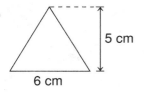

6 cm
5 cm

Area = _____

2.

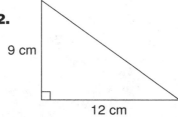

9 cm
12 cm

Area = _____

3.

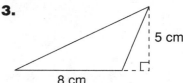

5 cm
8 cm

Area = _____

4. $b = 5.4$ cm
$h = 0.9$ cm

Area = _____

5. $b = 8.4$ cm
$h = 4$ cm

Area = _____

6. $b = 36$ m
$h = 12$ m

Area = _____

7. $b = 2.1$ m
$h = 0.08$ m

Area = _____

8. $b = 46$ cm
$h = 19$ cm

Area = _____

9. $b = 15$ m
$h = 10$ m

Area = _____

Use the formula $A = \frac{1}{2}h(b_1 + b_2)$ to find the area of each trapezoid.

10.

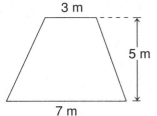

3 m
5 m
7 m

Area = _____

11.

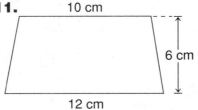

10 cm
6 cm
12 cm

Area = _____

12.

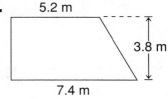

5.2 m
3.8 m
7.4 m

Area = _____

13. $b_1 = 10$ m
$b_2 = 15$ m
$h = 8$ m

Area = _____

14. $b_1 = 4.6$ km
$b_2 = 8.2$ km
$h = 7$ km

Area = _____

15. $b_1 = 50$ cm
$b_2 = 40$ cm
$h = 10$ cm

Area = _____

Name _____

Area of Circles

Use the formula $A = \pi r^2$ to find the approximate
area of each circle. Use a calculator.
Use 3.14 for π.

1.

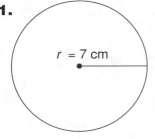

$r = 7$ cm

_____

2.

$d = 6.4$ cm

_____

3. $r = 21$ m   _____   **4.** $d = 12$ mm   _____

5. $d = 20$ km   _____   **6.** $r = 5$ cm   _____

7. $d = 8.2$ km   _____   **8.** $r = 0.5$ cm   _____

9. $r = 42$ km   _____   **10.** $d = 12.6$ m   _____

11. $r = 9.2$ mm   _____   **12.** $d = 0.2$ mm   _____

13. $d = 78$ cm   _____   **14.** $r = 100$ m   _____

15. $r = 17.5$ m   _____   **16.** $r = 84$ cm   _____

17. $r = 10.2$ m   _____   **18.** $d = 2,000$ km   _____

Name _____

Area of Irregular Shaped Figures

Use 3.14 for π when needed.
Find the area of each shaded region.

1.
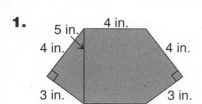
5 in. 4 in. 4 in. 4 in. 3 in. 3 in.

Area = _____

2.
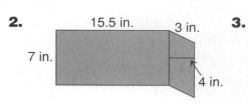
15.5 in. 3 in. 7 in. 4 in.

Area = _____

3.
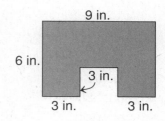
9 in. 6 in. 3 in. 3 in. 3 in.

Area = _____

4.
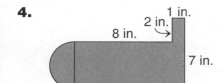
1 in. 2 in. 8 in. 7 in. 9 in.

Area = _____

5.
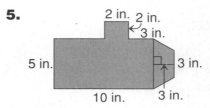
2 in. 2 in. 3 in. 5 in. 3 in. 10 in. 3 in.

Area = _____

6.
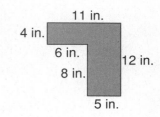
11 in. 4 in. 6 in. 12 in. 8 in. 5 in.

Area = _____

7.
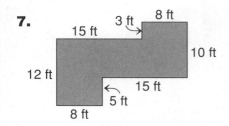
3 ft 8 ft 15 ft 10 ft 12 ft 15 ft 5 ft 8 ft

Area = _____

8.
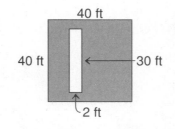
40 ft 40 ft 30 ft 2 ft

Area = _____

9.
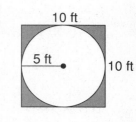
10 ft 5 ft 10 ft

Area = _____

10.
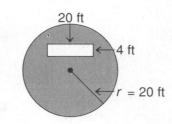
12 in. 7 in. 3 in. 5 in.

Area = _____

11.
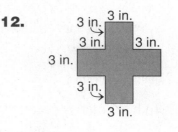
20 ft 4 ft r = 20 ft

Area = _____

12.
3 in. 3 in. 3 in. 3 in. 3 in. 3 in. 3 in.

Area = _____

Developing a Plan

Using the strategies, develop a plan and solve the problems.

1. For the first 10 years Mr. Singleton worked, he had 2 weeks vacation per year. For the next 4 years he had 3 weeks vacation per year. For the last 10 years he has had 4 weeks vacation per year. What is the average number of weeks vacation Mr. Singleton has had over the past 24 years?

_____

2. There are 32 players in an elimination table tennis tournament. The winner of each game plays another winner; the loser is eliminated. How many games must be played to determine the champion?

_____

3. Brenda, Robert, Sam, and Kathy are going to the movies together. How many ways can they sit in one row if Sam and Brenda do not sit next to each other?

_____

4. Ben starts a savings account with $24. His father will put $3 in the savings account for each additional $2 Ben deposits. If Ben saves $6 a week, in how many weeks will his savings be more than $100?

_____

In how many weeks will Ben's father have put as much money into the account as Ben?

_____

Name _____

Using Critical Thinking

Use the given dimensions to compare the areas.

1. The areas of how many circles with a radius of 9 in. are needed to equal the area of a circle with a radius of 18 in.?

_____

2. The areas of how many circles with a diameter of 2 cm are needed to equal the area of a circle with a diameter of 10 cm?

_____

3. It would take the areas of 4 circles with a radius of 8 cm to equal the area of one circle with a radius of

_____

4. It would take the areas of 49 circles with a radius of 3 m to equal the area of one circle with a radius of

_____

5. The area of one circle with a radius of 36 m will equal the areas of 9 circles with a radius of

_____

6. The area of one circle with a radius of 28 in. will equal the areas of 16 circles with a radius of

_____

Use >, <, or = to compare the areas.

7. Two circles with radius 7 mm $\bigcirc$ One circle with radius 14 mm

8. One circle with radius 5 in. and another circle with radius 3 in. $\bigcirc$ One circle with radius 6 in.

9. Three circles with diameter 5 ft $\bigcirc$ One circle with diameter 8 ft

10. Four circles with diameter 3 cm $\bigcirc$ One circle with diameter 6 cm

Name _____

Exploring Algebra: Solving a Formula for a Given Variable

Find the missing dimensions.

1.

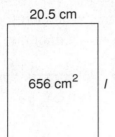

20.5 cm

656 cm^2 l

_____

2.

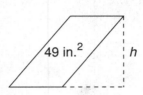

49 in.^{2} h

_____

3.

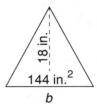

18 in.

144 in.^{2}

b

_____

4.

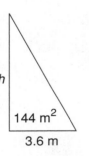

h

144 m^2

3.6 m

_____

5.

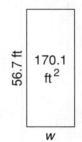

56.7 ft

170.1 ft^2

w

_____

6.

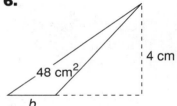

4 cm

48 cm^2

b

_____

7.

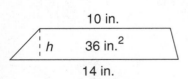

10 in.

h 36 in.^{2}

14 in.

_____

8.

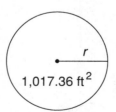

r

1,017.36 ft^2

_____

9.

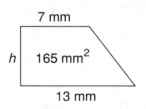

7 mm

h 165 mm^2

13 mm

_____

Name _____

Surface Area of Prisms and Cylinders

Find the surface area of each figure.

1.

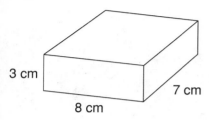

3 cm
8 cm
7 cm

Surface area _____

2.

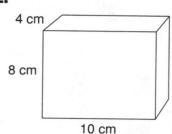

4 cm
8 cm
10 cm

Surface area _____

3.

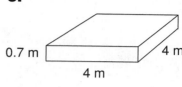

0.7 m
4 m
4 m

Surface area _____

4. $l = 12$ cm
   $w = 3.5$
   $h = 5$ cm

Surface area _____

5. $l = 5$ m
   $w = 1.5$ m
   $h = 2$ m

Surface area _____

6. $l = 3.6$ m
   $w = 2$ m
   $h = 0.8$ m

Surface area _____

7.

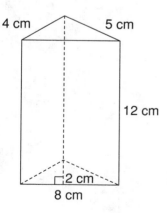

4 cm   5 cm
12 cm
2 cm
8 cm

Surface area _____

8.

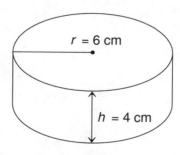

$r = 6$ cm
$h = 4$ cm

Surface area _____

9.

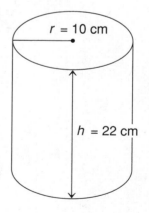

$r = 10$ cm
$h = 22$ cm

Surface area _____

10. $r = 6$ cm
    $h = 15$ cm

Surface area _____

11. $r = 3$ cm
    $h = 2.5$ cm

Surface area _____

12. $r = 11$ cm
    $h = 6$ cm

Surface area _____

Exploring the Concept of Volume

Find the volume of each figure. The hidden back view looks like the corner of a box.

1.

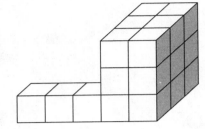

$V = $ _____

2.

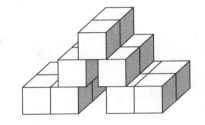

$V = $ _____

3.

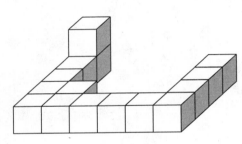

$V = $ _____

4.

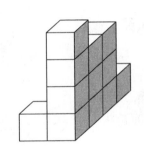

$V = $ _____

5.

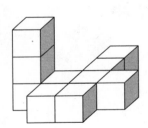

$V = $ _____

6.

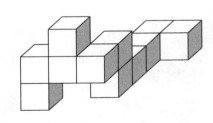

$V = $ _____

7.

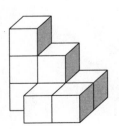

$V = $ _____

8.

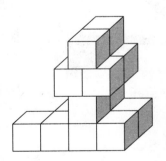

$V = $ _____

Volume of Prisms

Find the volume for each rectangular prism.
Use the formula $V = lwh$.

1.

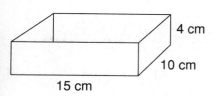

4 cm
10 cm
15 cm

V = _____

2.

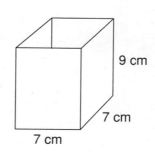

9 cm
7 cm
7 cm

V = _____

3.

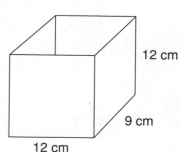

12 cm
9 cm
12 cm

V = _____

4. $l = 6.5$ mm
$w = 4.2$ mm
$h = 3.0$ mm

V = _____

5. $l = 2$ m
$w = 0.8$ m
$h = 1.5$ m

V = _____

6. $l = 20$ cm
$w = 15$ cm
$h = 12$ cm

V = _____

Find the volume of each prism.
Use the formula $V = bh$.

7.

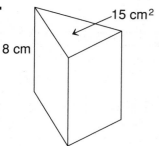

15 cm²
8 cm

V = _____

8. 5 mm

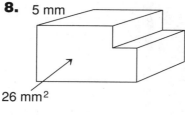

26 mm²

V = _____

9.

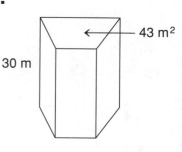

43 m²
30 m

V = _____

10. $B = 3.4$ m²
$h = 26$ m

V = _____

11. $B = 0.82$ m²
$h = 4.1$ m

V = _____

12. $B = 406$ mm²
$h = 52$ mm

V = _____

Name _____

Volume of a Cylinder

Use the formula $V = \pi r^2 h$ to find the volume of
each cylinder. Use 3.14 for π.

1.
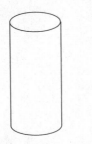

$r = 3$ cm
$h = 12$ cm
Volume ≈ _____

2.

$r = 7$ mm
$h = 7$ mm
Volume ≈ _____

3.

$r = 1$ cm
$h = 9$ cm
Volume ≈ _____

4.
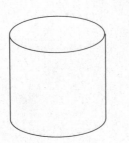

$r = 4$ cm
$h = 7$ cm
Volume ≈ _____

5.
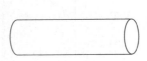

$r = 1$ dm
$h = 6$ dm
Volume ≈ _____

6.
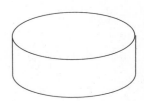

$r = 5$ mm
$h = 3$ mm
Volume ≈ _____

7.
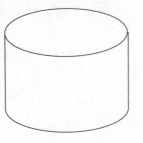

$r = 5$ cm
$h = 6$ cm
Volume ≈ _____

8.
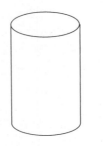

$r = 2$ cm
$h = 6$ cm
Volume ≈ _____

9.
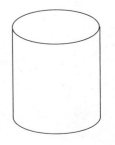

$r = 10$ mm
$h = 20$ mm
Volume ≈ _____

Name _____

Volume of Pyramids and Cones

Find the volume of each figure.

1.
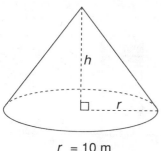

$r = 10$ m
$h = 16$ m

2.
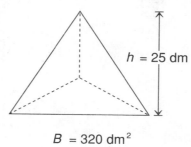

$h = 25$ dm

$B = 320$ dm^2

3.
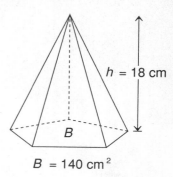

$h = 18$ cm

B

$B = 140$ cm^2

_____   _____   _____

4. cone

$r = 9$ in.
$h = 4$ in.

5. pyramid

$B = 14.2$ m^2
$h = 2.8$ m

6. pyramid

$B = 125$ cm^2
$h = 5.5$ cm

_____   _____   _____

7. cone

$r = 12$ ft
$h = 5$ ft

8. pyramid

$B = 2,588$ in.^{2}
$h = 6.4$ in.

9. pyramid

$B = 188.92$ m^2
$h = 10.1$ m

_____   _____   _____

10. cone

$r = 0.7$ m
$h = 2.2$ m

11. pyramid

$B = 346$ cm^2
$h = 12.9$ cm

12. pyramid

$B = 0.67$ ft^2
$h = 0.8$ ft

_____   _____   _____

Data from a Blueprint

Use the data from the blueprint to solve the problems.

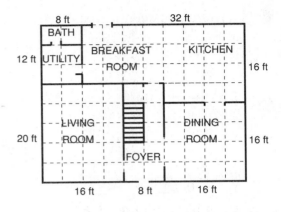

1. What is the area of the dining room?

_____

2. How much molding will be needed to go around the perimeter of the living room ceiling?

_____

3. How much greater is the perimeter of the living room than the perimeter of the dining room?

_____

4. If Mrs. Vaughn purchases 360 square feet of wall-to-wall carpet for the living room, how much will she have left over?

_____

5. Thirty-two square feet of the foyer floor are covered by the stairs. How many square feet of tile are needed for the rest of the foyer floor?

_____

6. What is the total area of the kitchen and the breakfast room?

_____

7. How many square feet of tile will be needed for the kitchen, breakfast room, bathroom, and utility room?

_____

8. The area of the bathroom is 32 square feet. What is the area of the utility room?

_____

9. What is the total area of the first floor of this house?

_____

10. How much greater than this would the area be if the width were increased by 3 feet and the length were increased by 5 feet?

_____

Name _____

Lines of Symmetry

Is the dotted line a line of symmetry? Write **yes** or **no**.

1.
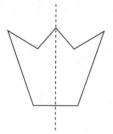
_____

2.
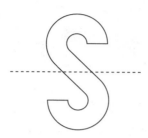

3.
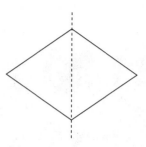
_____

4.
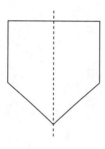
_____

5.
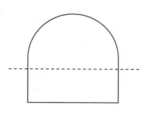

6.
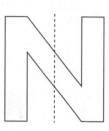
_____

Draw all the lines of symmetry.

7.
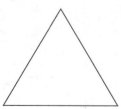

8.

9.
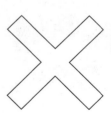

10.

11.
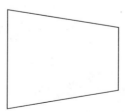

12.

Reflection in a Line

Draw the reflection image of each in line *l*.

1.

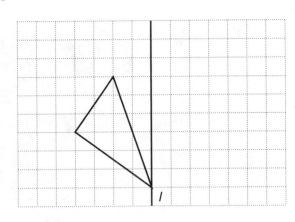

2.

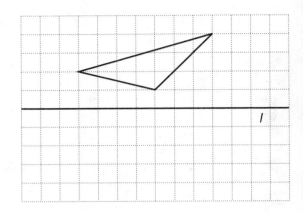

3.

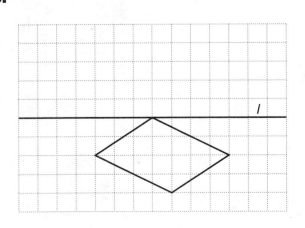

4.

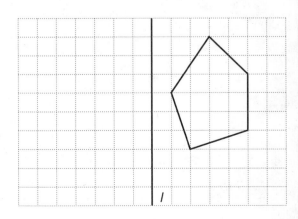

5.

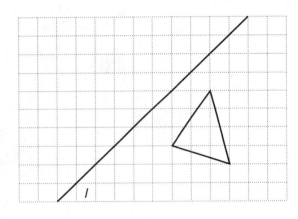

6.

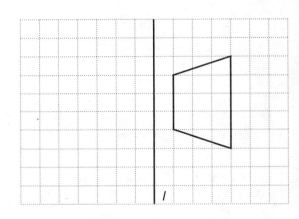

Turn Symmetry

Does the figure have turn symmetry?

1.

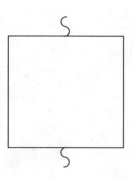

_____

2.

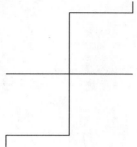

_____

3.

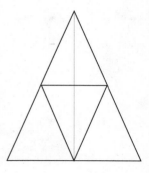

_____

The turn symmetry of each figure is what fraction of a full turn?

4.

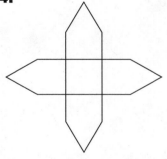

_____

5.

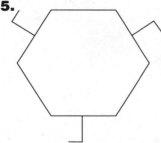

_____

6.

_____

7.

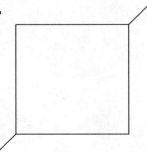

_____

8.

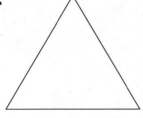

_____

9.

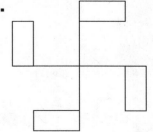

_____

Name _____

Rotations

Draw the $\frac{1}{2}$ turn image of each figure.

1.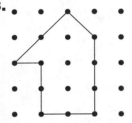

2.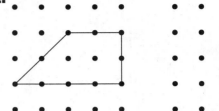

3.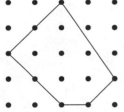

4.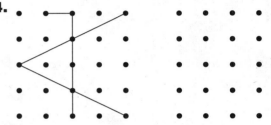

Draw the $\frac{1}{4}$ turn image of each figure.

5.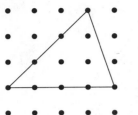

6.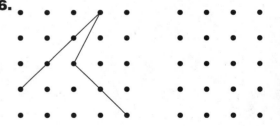

7.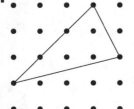

8.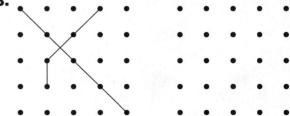

Name _____

Exploring Algebra: More Patterns and Functions

Complete each table.

1.

x	0	1	2	3
$y = x^2 + 2$				

2.

x	0	5	10	15
$y = x^2 + 2x$				

3.

x	2	10	200	500
$y = 2x + 5$				

4.

x	0	5	10	20
$y = x^2 + x - 1$				

5.

x	0	3	10	50
$y = 4x^2 + x + 1$				

6.

x	2	6	8	15
$y = 2x^2 + x - 1$				

Make a table showing 4 solutions for each equation.

7. $y = 3x^2 + 2x - 3$

8. $y = x^2 + x + 10$

9. $y = 4x^2 + x + 3$

10. $y = 5x^2 + 2x - 11$

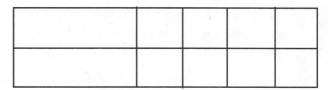

11. $y = |x| - 2$

12. $y = 2x \div 2$

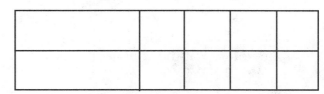

Name _____

Using the Strategies

Solve. Use any problem-solving strategy.

1. A rectangular container is 30 cm long, 22 cm wide, and 12 cm high. What is the volume of the container?

_____

What happens to the volume of the container if you double both the length and the width?

_____

2. A square container has a length of 3 m, a width of 3 m, and a height of 3 m. What is the volume of the container?

_____

What happens to the volume of the container if the height is doubled?

_____

3. A cylindrical tank is 20 ft high and 12 ft in diameter. If the diameter of the tank is changed to 24 ft, what happens to the volume?

_____

4. A circular swimming pool is filled to the 6-ft mark. The diameter of the pool is 20 ft. If the depth of water is decreased to 3 ft, what happens to the volume of water?

_____

5. A paper drinking cup shaped like a cone has a height of 10 cm. The diameter of the base is 6 cm. What is the volume of the cup?

_____

6. A rectangular fish tank holds 160 gallons of water. The volume of 1 gallon of water is 0.134 cu ft. What is the volume of the fish tank?

_____

7. A rectangular container is 95 cm long, 40 cm wide, and 50 cm high. What is the volume of the container?

_____

What happens to the volume if the width is doubled?

_____

8. What is the volume of a square scuba-diving pool if the pool is 30 ft on each side and 30 ft deep?

_____

What is the volume of liquid if there are only 15 ft of water in the pool?

_____

Name _____

Translations

Describe each slide.

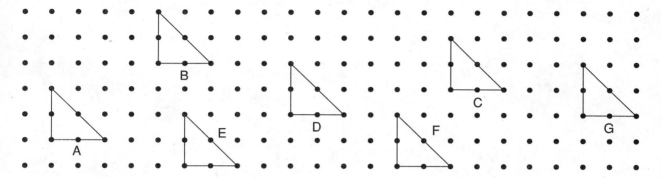

1. A to B

_____

2. E to D

_____

3. B to C

_____

4. E to F

_____

5. G to B

_____

6. C to D

_____

Draw the given slide image of each figure.

7. (2 down, 2 right)

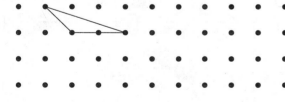

8. (2 up, 3 left)

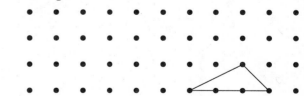

9. (3 left, 2 down)

10. (5 right, 2 up)

Motions and Congruence

Are the figures congruent? If so, what motion or combination of motions moves one figure onto another?

1.

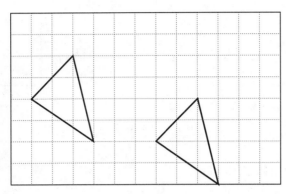

2.

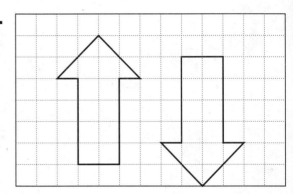

3.

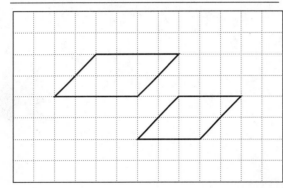

4.

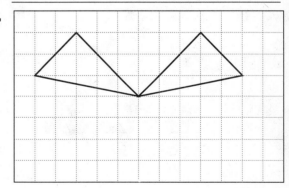

5.

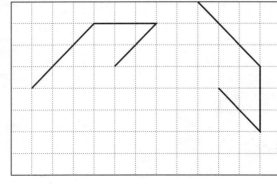

6.

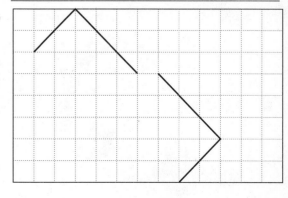

Using Critical Thinking

Find how many ways each figure can be divided
into 2 equal parts. List the assumptions you make.

1. You can divide this figure into 2 equal parts

in _____ way(s).

Assumptions: _____

_____

_____

_____

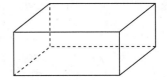

2. You can divide this figure into 2 equal parts

in _____ way(s).

Assumptions: _____

_____

_____

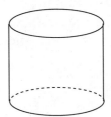

3. You can divide this figure into 2 equal parts

in _____ way(s).

Assumptions: _____

_____

_____

_____

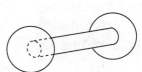

4. You can divide this figure into 2 equal parts

in _____ way(s).

Assumptions: _____

_____

_____

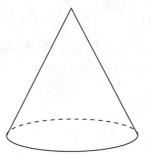

Estimating the Answers

Before solving the problem, estimate the answer.
Then solve the problem and decide if your answer
is reasonable.

1. In Mr. Ballo's math class, 12% of
his 25 students received an A.
How many students received an A?

Estimate: _____

Actual: _____

2. Jackie bowled 127, 142, 151, 133,
and 166. What was Jackie's average
for these 5 games?

Estimate: _____

Actual: _____

3. The Green Sports store is offering a
25% discount on all baseball equipment.
A glove regularly sells for $89.99.
What is the sale price of the glove?

Estimate: _____

Actual: _____

4. Cindy borrowed $560 for 1 year.
If the bank charges 12% annual interest
on a loan, how much does Cindy have
to pay the bank?

Estimate: _____

Actual: _____

5. A survey found that 325 out of 800
households have home computers.
What percent of those surveyed have
home computers?

Estimate: _____

Actual: _____

6. A survey of 600 households found
that 56% have VCRs. How many of
the houses surveyed have VCRs?

Estimate: _____

Actual: _____

7. Jack bought jeans for $35.99 and a
sweatshirt for $19.99. The tax was
$4.12. How much did Jack spend?

Estimate: _____

Actual: _____

8. Georgette worked 7 hours each day
for 5 days. She earned $262.50.
How much did she earn per hour?

Estimate: _____

Actual: _____

Name _____

Extending Order of Operations

Evaluate each numerical expression.

1. $3 \cdot 4 - 5$ _____

2. $(2 \cdot 5) + (4 \cdot 3)$ _____

3. $5 + 3 (3 - 4)^2$ _____

4. $(35 + 7) \div 6 + 3$ _____

5. $36 \div 6 \div 3$ _____

6. $40 - 10 \div 5 + 6$ _____

7. $137.2 - 21.3 \cdot 2$ _____

8. $12 \cdot 3 (11.1 + 6.5)$ _____

9. $(5 + 3) \div (10 - 6)$ _____

10. $3^4 \div 3 + 2 - 1$ _____

11. $2 \cdot (3 + 4)^2$ _____

12. $(2 + 1)^2 + (4 - 5)^2$ _____

13. $4 + 5 + 2^3$ _____

14. $(19 - 7) \cdot (4 + 8) + 8$ _____

Evaluate each algebraic expression.

15. $3 (6 + a)$ for $a = 4$

_____

16. $x + 9 \cdot 4 \div 2$ for $x = 3$

_____

17. $12 + (9 - 3) \div q$ for $q = 2$

_____

18. $36 - y^2 \div 2$ for $y = 8$

_____

19. $6h^2 - 2 \cdot 3 + 7$ for $h = 4$

_____

20. $12 + (w^2 - 3) \div 2$ for $w = 9$

_____

Write and evaluate an expression for each statement.

21. Add 12 to the product of 3 and $^-2$.

_____

22. Subtract 5 from 11 and then divide by 2.

_____

23. Multiply 11 and 3 and then subtract the product from 40.

_____

Using Guess and Check to Solve Equations

Solve. Use Guess and Check.

1. A car rental company charges $60 a day plus $9 for each additional hour past 24 hours. Mr. Harris owes the company $105. How many hours past 1 day did he use the car?

   Let n = number of hours past 24 hours.
   Solve: $9n + 60 = 105$

   _____

2. Mr. Manzo took his grandchildren to the zoo. The cost of tickets is $4 for adults and $2 for children. The total cost of admission was $20. How many children did Mr. Manzo take to the zoo?

   Let n = number of children.
   Solve: $2n + 4 = 20$

   _____

3. The Bayone Choir is performing in Harpersville. The choir is riding in 2 vans. Twenty choir members are riding in the first van. This is 4 less than twice the number riding in the second van. How many people are riding in the second van?

   Let n = number riding in van 2.
   Solve: $2n - 4 = 20$

   _____

4. To rent a movie at Anita's Video World costs $2 for the first night. Each additional night costs $3. Amanda rented a movie. The total cost of the rental was $11. How many additional nights did Amanda keep the movie?

   Let n = additional nights.
   Solve: $3n + 2 = 11$

   _____

5. The best-selling item in Jake's Deli is the hoagie sandwich. On Monday, Jake sold 56 sandwiches. This was 8 more than twice the amount he sold on Tuesday. How many sandwiches did Jake sell on Tuesday?

   Let n = number sold on Tuesday.
   Solve: $2n + 8 = 56$

   _____

6. On Thursday the temperature was 76°F. The temperature on Thursday was 24° less than twice the temperature on Wednesday. What was the temperature on Wednesday?

   Let n = temperature on Wednesday.
   Solve: $2n - 24 = 76$

   _____

7. Michael spent $16 on supplies for his science fair project. This is $6 less than twice the amount Jessica spent. How much did Jessica spend?

   Let n = amount Jessica spent.
   Solve: $2n - 6 = 16$

   _____

8. A band has 3 shows on Friday. This is 9 less than 4 times as many shows as it has on Saturday. How many shows are on Saturday?

   Let n = number of shows on Saturday.
   Solve: $4n - 9 = 3$

   _____

Name _____

Using Inverse Operations

Show how to build and undo each expression.

1. $7x - 2$

Build: Undo:

Start with x. _____   Start with $7x - 2$. _____

Multiply by 7. _____   Add 2. _____

Subtract 2. _____   Divide by 7. _____

2. $15y + 7$

Build: Undo:

_____   _____

_____   _____

_____   _____

3. $\frac{x}{5} + 8$

Build: Undo:

_____   _____

_____   _____

_____   _____

4. $\frac{w}{4} - 3.7$

Build: Undo:

_____   _____

_____   _____

_____   _____

Solving Two–step Equations

Solve and check.

1. $3n + 4 = 22$ _____

2. $5r + 3 = 33$ _____

3. $2x + 8 = 20$ _____

4. $6n + 8 = 38$ _____

5. $\frac{q}{3} + 6 = 18$ _____

6. $7m + 6 = 6$ _____

7. $\frac{b}{10} + 23 = 40$ _____

8. $\frac{w}{4} - 9 = 2$ _____

9. $2y + 15 = 31$ _____

10. $8t + 5 = 77$ _____

11. $^-7d + 7 = {}^-7$ _____

12. $4t - 42 = {}^-18$ _____

13. $^-12s - 48 = 12$ _____

14. $6w + 15 = 9$ _____

15. $\frac{x}{5} - 3 = 1$ _____

16. $\frac{x}{5} + 7 = 8$ _____

17. $\frac{3t}{4} - 1 = 2$ _____

18. $10y + 50 = 170$ _____

19. $4r - 6 = 14$ _____

20. $18m - 8 = 82$ _____

21. $9y + 10 = 1$ _____

22. $^-8n + 2 = 34$ _____

23. $5s + 1 = 21$ _____

24. $9t - 4 = 5$ _____

25. $\frac{x}{6} - 11 = {}^-10$ _____

26. $10m - 10 = {}^-3$ _____

27. $d + 15 = 23$ _____

28. $12 - 4y = {}^-8$ _____

29. $3s - 9 = 27$ _____

30. $4t - 3 = 5$ _____

Use the distributive property to help solve these
equations. Show your work.

31. $5(12 - x) = 50$

32. $\frac{1}{3}(12 + y) = 22$

_____   _____

Inventing Activities with a Function Machine

Use the given rule and output numbers to find the
input numbers.

1. $4x - 5$; output: 7, 31, 55

_____

2. $2x \div 2$; output: 3, 12, 50

_____

3. $12x \div 4$; output: 6, 51, 108

_____

4. $5x + 12$; output: 52, 127, 512

_____

5. $25x - 8$; output: 17, 292, 617

_____

6. $9x \div 5$; output: 18, 45, 90

_____

7. $13x \div 4$; output: 13, 52, 117

_____

8. $8 + 7x$; output: 43, 99, 148

_____

Look at the given input/output pairs and write a
rule for the function machine.

9.

input	output
2	7
7	17
10	23

Rule: _____

10.

input	output
3	6
15	66
30	141

Rule: _____

11.

input	output
12	12
100	100
500	500

Rule: _____

12.

input	output
10	91
20	181
30	271

Rule: _____

13.

input	output
1	8
2	10
3	12

Rule: _____

14.

input	output
16	28
36	63
60	105

Rule: _____

Graphing Inequalities

Write an inequality for each sentence.

1. The number of students (s) is less than 30.

_____

2. The temperature (t) is more than 52°F.

_____

3. Joe has an amount of money (m) at least $10.

_____

4. The depth (d) is no more than 10 feet above sea level.

_____

5. The savings (s) are between $45 and $100.

_____

6. The temperature (t) is more than 60°F but less than 80°F.

_____

Graph each inequality.

7. $^-5 < y$

```
<-+--+--+--+--+--+--+->
 ⁻9 ⁻8 ⁻7 ⁻6 ⁻5 ⁻4 ⁻3
```

8. $t > 20$

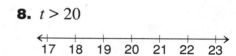

9. $k > 5.7$

```
<-+--+--+--+--+--+--+->
  3  4  5  6  7  8  9
```

10. $h \leq {}^-2\frac{1}{4}$

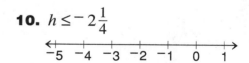

11. $^-3 < y < 8$

```
<-+-+-+-+-+-+-+-+-+-+-+-+->
⁻5⁻4⁻3⁻2⁻1 0 1 2 3 4 5 6 7 8
```

12. $6 \geq x > {}^-1$

```
<-+--+--+--+--+--+--+->
 ⁻1  0  1  2  3  4  5  6
```

13. $4 > t \geq 12$

```
<-+-+-+-+-+-+-+-+-+-+-+-+-+->
 2 3 4 5 6 7 8 9 10 11 12 13 14 15
```

14. $2 \leq s \leq 7\frac{1}{2}$

```
<-+--+--+--+--+--+--+->
  1  2  3  4  5  6  7  8
```

15. $^-12 < x \leq {}^-4$

```
<-+--+--+--+--+--+--+--+--+--+--+->
⁻14⁻13⁻12⁻11⁻10⁻9⁻8⁻7⁻6⁻5⁻4⁻3⁻2
```

16. $t \leq {}^-2.25$

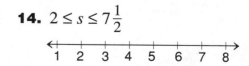

Solving Inequalities

Solve and check.

1. $r + 4 > {}^-1$ _____

2. $g - 3 < {}^-1$ _____

3. $x - 2 < {}^-2$ _____

4. $m - 6 \leq 2$ _____

5. ${}^-6 + y < {}^-8$ _____

6. $n - 4 \geq 3$ _____

7. $q + 4 \geq 3$ _____

8. $t - 9 < {}^-15$ _____

9. $r - 6 \leq {}^-3$ _____

10. $y + 4 > 6$ _____

11. $r - 47 > {}^-43$ _____

12. $12 + t \leq 6$ _____

13. $s + 15 \leq 18$ _____

14. $q - 12 > {}^-4$ _____

15. ${}^-8 + t \leq 6$ _____

16. ${}^-7 + r \geq 0$ _____

17. $w - 21 > {}^-3$ _____

18. $t - 14 < {}^-8$ _____

19. $s - 9 \geq 17$ _____

20. $y - 37 > 48$ _____

21. $t - 32 < 21$ _____

22. $m + 18 > 4$ _____

23. $r + 52 \geq 100$ _____

24. $x - 3 \leq {}^-9$ _____

25. $y - 4 < {}^-1$ _____

26. $t + 3 < {}^-3$ _____

27. $r + 6 < {}^-1$ _____

28. $m + 4 \geq 11$ _____

29. $m - 8 < 10$ _____

30. $t + 22 \geq 12$ _____

Equivalent Expressions

Write an equivalent expression.

1. $(3x + 4) + (2x + 1)$ _____   **2.** $x + 2x + 3 + 5$ _____

3. $(2x + 6) + (4x + 1)$ _____   **4.** $2(x + 3)$ _____

5. $4(3x + 2)$ _____   **6.** $3 + 2x + 5x + 1$ _____

7. $2 + 5x + 3 + 4x$ _____   **8.** $6(2x + 3)$ _____

9. $5(x + 12)$ _____   **10.** $6x + 1 + 9x$ _____

11. $(3x + 1) + (20 + x)$ _____   **12.** $5x + 1 + 2x + 9$ _____

13. $4x + 5x + 6x$ _____   **14.** $2 + 9 + x + 2x$ _____

15. $2(x + 1) + 4x$ _____   **16.** $3(4x + 2) + 8$ _____

17. $3x + (2x + 1)$ _____   **18.** $3x + 2x + x$ _____

19. $2(3x + 5) + 3(x + 1)$ _____   **20.** $7 + 9x + 4x$ _____

21. $x(8 + 2)$ _____   **22.** $2x + 3x + 7$ _____

23. $12x + 2 + 3x$ _____   **24.** $x + x + 11$ _____

25. $4x + x + (2x + 1)$ _____   **26.** $6x + (2x + 9) + 12$ _____

27. $9x + 2x + 3x$ _____   **28.** $2 + 5x + 7 + 8x$ _____

29. $(4x + 5) + (x + 12)$ _____   **30.** $(6x + 2)3 + 4(x + 1)$ _____

Inductive Reasoning: Discovering Number Patterns

1. How many dots would be in the 45th picture? _____

Fill in the next numbers in each pattern.

2.

1	4	7	10	13			

3.

1	3	7	15				

4.

2	5	14	41				

5.

2	4	6	8				

6.

4	16	36					

7.

2	8	18					

8.

3	5	7	9				

9.

9	25						

10.

6	20	42					

What is the sum of the first 10 square numbers?

Complete the table to find it. _____

Number	1	2	3	4	...	10
Square	1	4		16	...	
Running Total	1	5	14		...	

Name _____

Inductive Reasoning:
Discovering Geometric Patterns

1. Find the number of same-size right triangles on an 8 × 8 board without drawing them.

_____

4

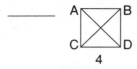

16

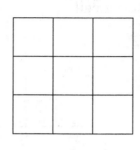

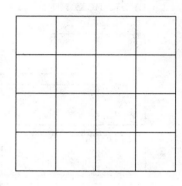

Draw pictures to help you find the patterns to answer these questions.

2. How many vertices would be shared by 3 or more lines if this figure were extended to 10 squares?

_____

2 + 3 + 4

3. How many vertices would be shared by 3 or more lines if the figure had 28 squares?

_____

Use the picture to find the pattern.

4. What is the perimeter of this figure?

_____

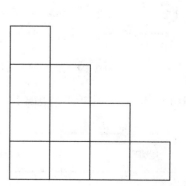

5. What would be the perimeter if this figure had 15 squares?

_____

6. If this figure had 28 squares?

Discovering Relationships

Study this method of dividing fractions.

$$\frac{8}{9} \div \frac{4}{3} = \frac{8 \div 4}{9 \div 3} = \frac{2}{3}$$

Use this method to do these exercises.

1. $\frac{12}{15} \div \frac{3}{5}$ _____

2. $\frac{16}{18} \div \frac{8}{9}$ _____

3. $\frac{14}{15} \div \frac{2}{3}$ _____

4. $\frac{14}{35} \div \frac{7}{5}$ _____

5. $\frac{16}{42} \div \frac{4}{6}$ _____

6. $\frac{12}{16} \div \frac{6}{4}$ _____

Do these exercises using the new method. Rename the dividend fraction if necessary.

7. $\frac{4}{7} \div \frac{2}{5}$ _____

8. $\frac{9}{11} \div \frac{3}{4}$ _____

9. $\frac{8}{12} \div \frac{3}{4}$ _____

10. $\frac{16}{20} \div \frac{2}{5}$ _____

11. $\frac{4}{5} \div \frac{2}{4}$ _____

12. $\frac{2}{5} \div \frac{2}{3}$ _____

13. $\frac{10}{25} \div \frac{4}{10}$ _____

14. $\frac{3}{4} \div \frac{5}{6}$ _____

Informal Proof in Algebra

Solve.

1. Eight students belong to a gymnastics club. To complete a rotation, each one must perform on 4 pieces of equipment. How many performances will be completed at the end of 2 rotations?

_____

2. If the same gymnastics club had n students, how many performances would be completed at the end of 3 rotations? _____

3. Eight friends exchanged birthday cards during the year. At the end of the year, how many cards had been exchanged?

_____

How many cards would be exchanged among n friends? _____

Try the number tricks below. Then write the steps that explain why each one works.

4. Pick any number. Add 4 to that number. Multiply your result by 6. Divide that answer by 2. Subtract 12. Finally, divide by 3. Is the answer your

number? _____

5. Choose a number. Multiply it by 7. Add 13 to the result. Multiply that answer by 2. Subtract 5. Divide that result by 7. Subtract 3. Divide that answer by your number. Is 2 your

final answer? _____

Informal Proof in Geometry

1. Each quadrilateral has been partitioned into
triangles by connecting vertices.

How many triangles are formed? _____
What is the sum of the measures of the angles of a

quadrilateral? _____

2. Partition each heptagon below completely
into triangles by connecting vertices.

  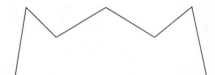

What is the total of the measures of the angles in

each heptagon? _____

3. Can the following figures be partitioned using the

same method? _____ Partition them.

A    **B**    **C**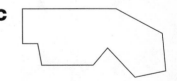

4. Use the information from Problems 1, 2, and 3
to complete the following chart.

Figure	Number of Sides	Number of Triangles	Sum of Measures of the Angles
Quadrilateral	4	2	2•180° or 360°
Heptagon	7	5	_____
A	_____	_____	_____
B	_____	_____	_____
C	_____	_____	_____

Language of Logic

Decide whether the compound statement in each case is true or false. Complete each table.

1.

P	Q	P or Q
True	True	
True	False	
False	True	
False	False	

2.

P	Q	P and Q
True	True	
True	False	
False	True	
False	False	

3.

P	Q	If P, then Q
True	True	
True	False	
False	True	
False	False	

Use the tables above to help you label each compound statement **true** or **false.**

4. $10 \div 2 = 5$ or $10 \div 2 = 3$.

_____

5. $3 \times 4 = 12$ and $3 \times 3 = 9$.

_____

6. $18 > 7$ and $7 < 6$.

_____

7. If $18 \div 9 = 2$, then $3 \times 4 = 12$.

_____

8. If $\frac{2}{3} \times \frac{3}{4} = \frac{1}{2}$, then $\frac{3}{4} \times 4 = 3$.

_____

9. $45 > 32$ and $32 > 44$.

_____

10. If $32 \div 2 = 7$, then $14 \div 7 = 2$.

_____

11. $20 \times 2 = 10$ or $12 \times 2 = 24$.

_____

12. x is a multiple of 2 or x is a multiple of 3.

_____

13. If x is a multiple of 2, then x is prime.

_____

Name _____

Logical Inference

Write the conclusion from chaining these A → B,
B → C statements.

1. If we arrive at school too early, the
doors will be locked. If the doors are
locked, we cannot enter the building.

_____

_____

_____

2. If the car will not start, we will miss
practice. If we miss practice, we will
miss tomorrow's game.

_____

_____

_____

3. If the rain stops, we will walk home.
If we walk home, we will visit the
library.

_____

_____

4. If n is an even number, it can be
divided by 2. If n can be divided by 2,
then it is not prime.

_____

_____

5. If $a = 1$, then $b = 2$.
If $b = 2$, then $c = 3$.

_____

6. If $a > b$, then $b > c$.
If $b > c$, then $a > c$.

_____

Look at each A → B statement. Then write
your own B → C statement and chain them.

7. If it is cold out, I will wear my new coat.

_____

_____

_____

8. If I finish my work, I will read my book.

_____

_____

_____

Reasoning from Graphs

Read the story, look at the graph, and answer the questions.

Kyle mowed the lawn on Saturday. He carefully started the mower and let it pick up speed as he moved away from the shed. He mowed the open area of the yard and began to slow down as he neared some bushes. After he mowed around the bushes, he picked up speed again. As he went around the side of the house the mower ran out of gas. His father helped him refill the tank. Then they restarted the mower and Kyle finished mowing the lawn.

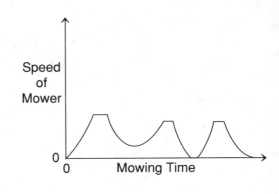

1. What is happening when the graph line is flat?

_____

2. What is happening when the graph line slopes down gradually?

_____

3. Put the letter A on the graph to show where Kyle mowed near the bushes.

4. Put the letter B on the graph to show where the mower ran out of gas.

5. Change the graph to show that Kyle stopped to rest for a while after he mowed near the bushes.

This story of a kite is not in the right order. Decide where each event happened. Then use the letters to label each event on the graph.

6. **A** The kite went higher when the wind increased.

7. **B** The kite was carried up very quickly.

8. **C** The kite hit the ground.

9. **D** The kite went no higher but drifted at that height.

10. **E** The kite fell a few feet when the wind slowed.

11. **F** The kite drifted down when the wind stopped.

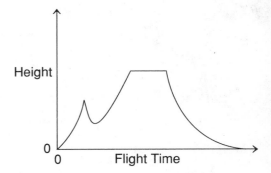

Solving Related Problems

Solve.

1. Alfredo, Ben, Jeff, and Kevin bought a model plane, a cassette, a shirt, and a jacket. Jeff bought nothing in the clothing store. Ben played his purchase on the way home. Kevin's purchase had short sleeves. What did each boy buy?

_____

_____

_____

2. The Yankees, Tigers, and Orioles all played one another twice in baseball. The Yankees won 3 of their games. The Orioles won 2 of theirs. What is each team's win/loss record?

_____

_____

3. A shirt costs $9.00 more than a tie. The total cost of both items is $24.50. What is the cost of the shirt? What is the cost of the tie?

_____

4. Carlos, Fred, and Randy drove to the out-of-town game, a distance of 376 miles. Randy drove twice as far as Carlos. Fred drove 3 times as far as Randy. How many miles did each person drive?

_____

_____

Menu			
Ham sandwich ----------------------- $2.30		Fruit salad --------------------------- $1.50	
Hamburger ---------------------------- 2.00		Potato salad --------------------------- 1.10	
Grilled cheese ------------------------ 1.85		Milk -------------------------------------- 0.65	
Chicken sandwich -------------------- 2.10		Fruit juice ----------------------------- 0.70	

5. Charley ordered a hamburger, potato salad, and a glass of milk. He paid with a $5 bill. How much change did he get?

_____

6. On Tuesday, 20% is deducted from the bill. Lee and Sue ordered a chicken sandwich, a grilled cheese, a fruit salad, and two juices. How much was their bill?

_____